PEACE OF MIND

BY

Joshua Loth Liebman

SIMON AND SCHUSTER, NEW YORK

THIRTY-FIRST PRINTING

MANUFACTURED IN THE UNITED STATES OF AMERICA
AMERICAN BOOK–STRATFORD PRESS, INC., NEW YORK

TO FAN,
MY BELOVED WIFE AND CO-WORKER

TABLE OF CONTENTS

Table of Contents

A WORD TO THE READER

IT MAY SEEM *strange for a man to write a book about peace of mind in this age of fierce turmoil and harrowing doubts. It may seem doubly strange for a rabbi, a representative of a people that has known so little peace, to engage in such an enterprise. However, I make no apologies for this attempt to find new answers to the basic problems of human nature: its needs, motives, fears, and dreams. I have written this book in the conviction that social peace can never be permanently achieved so long as individuals engage in civil war with themselves. I maintain that a co-operative world can never be fashioned by men and women who are corroded by the acids of inner hate, and I believe that our much-heralded "society of security" will remain a Utopian vision so long as the individuals composing that society are desperately insecure, not only economically but emotionally and spiritually.*

In this book I try to present some answers that have proved helpful to me about the universal human dilemmas of conscience, love, fear, grief, and God—crucial problems that present themselves in every kind of society, and, I believe, will present themselves as long as man is man.

Now it is undoubtedly true that social circumstances do profoundly modify our human responses, and that unjust economic conditions do create neuroses and maladjustments in countless personalities. Social reformers and revolutionaries are right when they insist that multitudes of human beings can never experience true peace of mind so long as

A Word to the Reader

they are compelled to engage in a relentless and too frequently defeating battle for work and bread. There is no question about it—a more just social order will cure vast numbers of people of their present inner conflicts and maladjustments.

Recognizing this truth, economic liberal and social radicals often accuse modern psychologists and religionists of merely pouring Listerine on a cancer, the cancer being economic exploitation. Remove the latter, they imply, and all psychic distortions will disappear. This appears to me as gross over-simplification. Certainly we must battle for a decent and just economic social order as the matrix of personal sanity and balance. When such an order is achieved many of our present day emotional ills will vanish. Yet in any kind of society certain universal psychological reactions will manifest themselves, certain emotional constants, as it were, will make their appearance, and men and women will have to learn then, as now, how to manage their psychic needs and conflicts with a greater artistry.

Whether under capitalism, socialism, or communism, men and women will still face the purely personal and profoundly individual issues of life and death as well as the tangled interpersonal relations of parent and child, brother and sister, husband and wife. In Moscow, London, or New York, the family is still the family and men and women have to learn how to understand and manage their feelings of hostility against family rivals and work-competitors, their moods of aggression, their reactions of fear in the presence of rejection or defeat. Thus while it is unquestionably true that we shall have a healthier human nature in a co-operative society than under a ruthlessly competitive system, yet grief will still re-

A Word to the Reader

main grief no matter what the social system, and hard-earned psychic wisdom will be prerequisite for human beings after bread has been won and status and security gained.

Many men far wiser than I are at work today planning social and economic change. For their creative labors, every thinking person must be grateful. We must join with them in the struggle to obtain a common victory for economic, industrial, and political democracy throughout the world. At the same time it should be recognized that the healthier society must be built by healthier human beings! *The average person is at moments consumed with feelings of guilt about his relations to those closest to him; he wants to love people but feels withdrawn, rigid, and somehow frozen. At other moments he grows afraid without knowing exactly why he is afraid; he is particularly confused and unhappy when he faces the loss of a loved one or confronts the thought of his own death. Many religious books only conspire to make him feel more guilty and more sinful while many psychological books, although trying to reassure him, merely add to his inner confusion by making him feel somehow that he is a "case history" in abnormal psychology. People keep their troubles and worries often too much to themselves because they do not know where to turn for wise guidance. Personal experience plus rich and varied contacts in my ministry led me to believe that a book written by a religionist explaining just what modern psychology has discovered about human beings, why we sometimes hate ourselves and hate others, why we grow afraid, why we lose faith in life and in God, might be of real help to perplexed moderns. This science also tells us what we can do to change ourselves and our mental*

A Word to the Reader

attitudes in relation to our own personalities and in inter-relations with other human beings.

This book attempts to distill the helpful insights about human nature that psychology has discovered and the encouraging news from the scientific clinic about man's infinite capacity to change and improve himself, as well as to correlate these latest scientific discoveries with the truest religious insights and goals of the ages.

J. L. L.

PEACE OF
MIND

CHAPTER ONE

Questing Inward

ONCE, as a young man full of exuberant fancy, I undertook to draw up a catalogue of the acknowledged "goods" of life. As other men sometimes tabulate lists of properties they own or would like to own, I set down my inventory of earthly desirables: health, love, beauty, talent, power, riches, and fame—together with several minor ingredients of what I considered man's perfect portion.

When my inventory was completed I proudly showed it to a wise elder who had been the mentor and spiritual model of my youth. Perhaps I was trying to impress him with my precocious wisdom and the large universality of my interests. Anyway, I handed him the list. "This," I told him confidently, "is the sum of mortal goods. Could a man possess them all, he would be as a god."

At the corners of my friend's old eyes, I saw wrinkles of amusement gathering in a patient net. "An excellent list," he said, pondering it thoughtfully. "Well digested in content and set down in not-unreasonable order. But it appears, my young friend, that you have omitted the most important element of all. You have forgotten the one ingredient lacking which each possession becomes a hideous torment, and your list as a whole an intolerable burden."

Peace of Mind

"And what," I asked, peppering my voice with truculence, "is that missing ingredient?"

With a pencil stub he crossed out my entire schedule. Then, having demolished my adolescent dream structure at a single stroke, he wrote down three syllables: *peace of mind.*

"This is the gift that God reserves for His special protégés," he said. "Talent and beauty He gives to many. Wealth is commonplace, fame not rare. But peace of mind—that is His final guerdon of approval, the fondest sign of His love. He bestows it charily. Most men are never blessed with it; others wait all their lives—yes, far into advanced age—for this gift to descend upon them."

He scanned the doubt on my young forehead. "This is no private opinion of mine," he explained. "I am merely paraphrasing from the Psalmists, Marcus Aurelius, and Lao-tse." (It was a favorite trick of his to assign his own hard-won wisdom to ancient teachers.) " 'God, Lord of the universe,' says each of these wise ones, 'heap worldly gifts at the feet of foolish men. But on my head pour only the sweet waters of serenity. Give me the gift of the Untroubled Mind.' "

At that time I found it difficult wholly to believe the wisdom of my rabbinic friend. But a quarter of a century of personal experience and professional observation has served only to confirm his almost oracular utterance. I have come to understand that peace of mind is the characteristic mark of God Himself, and that it has always been the true goal of the considered life. I know now that the sum of all other possessions does not necessarily add up to peace of mind; yet, on the other hand, I have seen this inner tranquillity flourish without the material supports of property or even the buttress of physical health. Slowly, painfully, I have learned that peace of mind may transform a cottage into a spacious manor hall; the want of it can make a regal park an imprisoning nutshell.

The quest for this unwearied inner peace is constant and universal. Probe deeply into the teachings of Buddha, Maimonides, or à Kempis, and you will discover that they base their diverse doctrines on the foundations of a large spiritual serenity. Analyze the prayers of troubled, overborne mankind of all creeds, in every age—and their petitions come down to the irreducible common denominators of daily bread and inward peace. Grown men do not pray for vain trifles. When they lift up their hearts and voices in this valley of tears they ask for strength and courage and understanding.

Especially today, when the prayers of men ascend, mourning and wailing to the Bestower of Gifts, they plead for an inward tranquillity that is both a fortress and a sanctuary. And with reason. Modern man is treading a narrow defile that skirts an Inferno of such destruction as Dante could not envision nor Doré depict. Stricken by psychic anxieties, cloven by emotional conflicts, beset by economic insecurities, assailed by political doubts and cynicisms, the plucked rooster, man, is a peculiarly vulnerable fowl as he struts along the path of civilization. He has crowed a good deal in his time, rather bravely in spots. But now he begins to suspect that the ax of destiny is being sharpened for his neck. He trembles, pales, calls for madder music, stronger wine to drown the approaching specter of his fate. For the fact emerges that contemporary man, like T. S. Eliot's fatigued and pitiful Prufrock, is afraid!

In his fear he casts about for devices and techniques of

Peace of Mind

salvation—something that will carry him through new dangers and give him sorely needed courage to face the old ones. What he needs (what we all need) is not a set of reassuring answers—for no such formula of reassurance exists—but rather an inner equilibrium, a spiritual stability that is proof against confusion and disaster. Peace of mind must not be identified with ivory-tower escapism from the hurly-burly of life, nor is it, as Whitehead points out, "a negative conception of anesthesia." Rather, it enables us to accept the pummelings of fate and fortune with equanimity—even with a kind of eagerness sprung of the sure knowledge that such buffetings cannot divert us from our creative life course.

Serious-minded social reformers ask in all sincerity: "Have men the *right* to peace of mind today? Is anyone morally justified even in contemplating this state when the world is in such a tumult of reconstruction?" We reply: "No reconstructed society can be built on unreconstructed individuals. Personal unbalance *never* leads to social stability. And peace of mind is the indispensable prerequisite of individual and social balance."

This shockproof balance must be achieved *inside* the soul. "Man must be arched and buttressed from within," says Marcus Aurelius, "else the temple wavers to the dust." But these sustaining arches can never be raised until the temple of man's soul is at peace with itself.

Quite an undertaking! Clearly, peace of mind is not something that can be bought in bottles, or applied like a cosmetic to the surface of the skin: it cannot be attained by taking a tablet before meals, or by enrolling for a "course" three evenings a week. I sometimes think that long and intimate association with noble works—literary, philosophic, artistic—is a splendid promoter of inward peace, but then I recall that many of the greatest savants and artists were pitifully restless men, driven relentlessly to the frantic completion of their appointed labors. No, intellectualism does not always confer peace of mind. Goethe's Faust—in many ways the archetype of troubled modern man—possessed a hard-earned mastery of science, philosophy, and mathematics, yet we know of the sorry bargain that this tormented hero made with the powers of evil in his search for contentment.

Occasionally, we are calmed by listening to the vast harmonies of Beethoven, or find fellow comfort in the twilight musings of Chopin. But these are merely occasional opiates; they lull us to repose when the inward stresses are too violent to be borne. A few fortunate persons can be soothed by the contemplation of an El Greco or the bucolic peace of a Constable. The balance of color, proportion, and the inward design of great paintings provide valuable clues to the condition of tranquillity. But because a painted canvas has only two dimensions (or possibly three) it cannot wholly satisfy the limitlessly unnumbered dimensions of the soul.

To what then shall we turn for instruction in the difficult art of being at peace with ourselves? Not to alcohol—though feverishly excessive drinking, a leprous scab on the contemporary soul, is apparently on the increase. Not to barbiturates —though increasing millions of grains are being swallowed by Americans in their search for sedative repose. Neither shall we find lasting solace in sensual indulgence, though all too many motion pictures and fantasy magazines glorify these activities as the be-all and end-all of life.

7

Peace of Mind

Certainly we shall not find peace in the race for fame—"that last infirmity of noble minds," as Milton terms it—nor in the furious pursuit of wealth which slips like quicksilver through our grasping fingers. Nor is tranquillity to be gained by summoning up the "thousand stupefying nothings" of an hour—for although they "benumb us at our call," the old restlessness returns as soon as we stop our waterbug dartings and chair-hoppings. And finally, not even in the sublime sharings of human love—that emotion which most powerfully conveys (and sometimes mars) the illusion of perfect happiness—is peace of mind reliably to be found.

Where then shall we look, at what bar shall we sue, what posture shall we take, what principle invoke, in this endless, basic, and all-important quest for peace of mind?

Worthy questions, deserving of thoughtful, sincere answers. The key to the problem, a simple enough instrument if only we dare use it, is to be found in Matthew Arnold's noble poem, *Empedocles on Etna*. Empedocles the Greek philosopher, soliloquizing atop the volcanic mountain, surveys the troubled world below, anatomizes man's griefs, brings all his faculties to the solution of the question which then, as now, canvassed the possibility of mortal contentment amidst scenes of immortal discontent. Empedocles, convinced that man is the maker of his own restless grief, coolly declares:

> *We would have inward peace*
> *But will not look within . . .*

But will not look within! Here, in a single phrase, our wilfullness is bared by the poet's ruthless incision. We are like stubborn invalids who know they are ill but will not accept the sharp prescription of cure. Hold the mirror up to our sallow complexions? Never! Such scrutiny would demand that we trace our symptoms inward to the sick source of our misery —our secret troubled soul. Unthinkable! Yet until we do so trace our malady, there can be no hope for recovery and we may as well resign ourselves to the half life of the coward and self-cheat.

Practically, it is not an easy matter to "look within." Techniques *do* exist however, and until quite recently religion seemed to have a monopoly on them. Spiritual meditation has always been the gateway to a special kind of self-knowledge, and, certainly, a rich reward awaits the contemplative soul that can commune with itself under the solitary laburnum of thought. Ancient Judaism understood the healing value of inner contemplation and devised many of its great holy days to serve as vehicles for the encouragement of self-communion and confession.

The Catholic Church has a serviceable device in its "examination of conscience"—the prerequisite of a good confession. Before the Catholic enters the confessional he scrutinizes the state of his soul and draws up a balance sheet in terms of sins—both of commission and omission. He is thus enabled to know how his moral accounts stand. The limitations of this technique will be discussed later; for the present, however, it must be admitted that auricular confession is a practical historic tool for probing certain portions of the soul.

Within the past half century, and rapidly within the last decade, there has been developed a new method of gaining insight into the deepest emotional and psychologic disturbances that threaten man's peace of mind. This new technique picneered by Sigmund Freud is a means of investigating the profound basic drives of men, and of discovering how, when, and why these fundamental energies have become diverted into neurotic channels.

Despite the ignorance and hostility of its opponents, dynamic psychology has made enormous strides; it is now recognized as an indispensable clinical tool in the treatment of many illnesses, mental and physical and emotional. I do not intend to give here even a brief description of this newest branch of therapeutic science, but wish merely to suggest that of all techniques yet devised for "looking within" it is the keenest and most revelatory of our true inner nature.

So shocking is the frankness with which the psychiatric mirror reveals our inward flaws and spiritual crevasses that many persons are hesitant about glancing into this unflattering glass. An erroneous impression has gotten abroad that psychoanalysis reveals man solely as a creature of base passions and low desires. Truth to tell, it *does* cast an embarrassingly bright beam upon our instinctual drives, our basic loves and hates. But this light is generated only to disperse the sickish fog of sentimentality that has clouded man's knowledge of himself. When we once realize that we are endowed with explosive energies as ruthless and amoral as the atomic bomb —we are at the beginning of our self-understanding. And when we discover that it is the triumph of psychology to translate these energies into constructive, beautiful forms—then, and then only, shall we be in a position to speak honestly and act honestly, on the hitherto sentimentally clouded subject of human nature.

Take, for example, our sentimental misconceptions about

Questing Inward

the chubby little gurgler in his crib. How innocent, how positively angelic, he appears as he coos engagingly under his mother's doting gaze. A little bundle of heaven he seems, and we vie with one another in ascribing to him the purest of emotions. But actually the chubby little darling has been revealed by modern psychology to be a bundle of powerful drives—of possessive love for his mother, of powerful inner rage in moments of inevitable frustration, of deep fears and uncertainty in facing a strange world, satisfying and frightening at one and the same moment. Toward his brothers, sisters, and father he develops a duality of emotions. He loves them; yes, but at the same time fears and even at moments furiously hates these rivals in the kingdom of love.

If this be a fairly accurate psychograph of an infant (and all psychologists agree that it is), how then shall we picture the awful complexities of the soul that has left the crib and nursery and has entered the arena of adolescence and adult life? How many fail and fall therein! How many are bewildered, self-maimed, and disfigured in the battle! As we observe the growing hordes of neurotics and little tyrants, self-mutilators and self-slayers, that trail about the world, we realize that a new, more honest, and more dynamic map of man's troubled soul must be drawn before we can hope to explore this most tangled of terrains.

Only one crayon can draw such a detailed map—and that is the crayon of modern psychology. Gazing steadily, unflinchingly, at our inward selves, we learn under the psychiatrist's guidance to draw the picture of our own soul. We learn to look upon our flaws and potentialities, and with searching fingers to probe out the causes of our failures, hates, and fears.

11

Peace of Mind

We find out who we are! Psychotherapy is a method by which we stop being someone we thought we were (or have been told we ought to be) and become *ourselves.* It is a technique by which we cease to be infants, crying for impossible moons of attainment. It is the compass that holds us to the true north of maturity and self-understanding, and this in turn enables us to accept disappointment, failure, rejection, even death, with adult peace of mind.

I do not mean to imply that there have not been other pathways to inner serenity than the road now opened by Freud and his successors. It would be absurd, nay impossible, to ignore the great and serene souls of the saints and mystics, the poets and philosophers, who achieved peace of mind by other disciplines. As a matter of fact, psychology alone is never enough for man's great adventure—life. Like all other sciences, it formulates no moral goal; it is not a philosophy of life, nor did its pioneers ever intend it to be. It is a *key* to the temple, not the temple itself. I believe that it must be supplemented by religion, and that only the blended light of these two great beacons will guide individuals and nations through the hazardous channels ahead.

By religion I mean the accumulated spiritual wisdom and ethical precepts dating from the time of the earliest Prophets and gradually formulated into a body of tested truth for man's moral guidance and spiritual at-homeness in the universe. Such religion alone can provide the emotional dynamics, the moral imperatives, by which the human race can progressively attain its individual and social fulfillments.

A wise religion is indispensable for peace of mind because it blesses us with inner gifts beyond the bestowal of any science: a sense of our purpose in the world, a feeling of related-ness to God, the shared warmth of group fellowship, and the subordination of our little egos to great moral and spiritual ends. Religion, at its best, is the announcer of the supreme ideals by which men must live and through which our finite species finds its ultimate significance. Yet honesty compels us to admit that religion needs help if it is to make these ideals incarnate in human life.

Psychology can become one of the real allies in that mag-nificent religious task. It can reveal why human goodness is still such a distant goal. Men who are inwardly tormented and emotionally unhappy can never be good partners of God; the great ideals of religion will remain unimplemented and un-fulfilled so long as unhappy, distorted men and women con-tinue to be defective transmitters of the Divine.

Dynamic psychology, created by Freud and developed by such present-day workers as Alexander, Horney, and Men-ninger, understands why human beings become "split souls," why they are so often cynical and cruel to themselves and to others. This priceless knowledge must be assimilated by modern religion if it wishes the human race to attain its goal of the good life. Unfortunately, however, many creeds have failed to keep pace with the changing needs of men. The rea-sons for this failure are not too obscure. Western religion was born in a pre-scientific, certainly a pre-psychological, era. I cer-tainly do not deny that the saints and philosophers of religion have often penetrated into the hidden chambers of the human heart and contributed many valuable intuitive insights. To-day, however, these insights must be richly supplemented by the illuminating and often startling new truths about human nature emerging from the psychological laboratory. A pre-psychological religion cannot satisfy mankind in its quest for salvation in this psychological age.

Religion, if it ignores creative psychiatry or in deprecating it, is in grave danger of losing a superb ally in the battle for the good life. This has happened to religion many times. Repeatedly throughout the ages it has resisted rather than welcomed new truths; as a result such sciences as astronomy, physics, and biology broke away from religion. Theologians too often made the mistake of believing that their particular formulations of God's word were the final revelation of His wisdom. Galileo was rejected by them because his fresh and deeper insight into God's laws did not coincide with theology's static and rigidly fixed conceptions.

Some religionists today are in a similar danger of rejecting the newest and sharpest tools that God has given men for the examination of the human mind and its complex motives. They acknowledge that science has the power of delving into the mysteries of astronomy and the composition of matter. But they maintain that in the realm of conduct and morals, religion must have the last word, even though that last word is rooted in an antiquated psychology.

But wiser religious teachers today are coming to see the fallacy of identifying truth with the frozen concepts of the past. They insist that whatever aids mankind in its quest for self-fulfillment is a new revelation of God's working in history, and that psychology's discoveries about conduct and motive are really the most recent syllables of the Divine.

If we are to find peace of mind today, religion must be not only willing but anxious to absorb the new insights into hu-

14

man motivation, the discoveries about man's drives and impulses, his hates and loves and fears, that come from the psychological clinic. Religion must not hesitate to use the microscope of psychology, with its depth analysis of the human mind. Nor should it indulge in homilies about the "necessity of character" at the very moment when the new soul science of psychology is liberating distorted individuals from their conflicts and cruelty, not by preaching, but by changing character.

Today's cringing world needs the support of a peace-giving faith that combines the substance of the old with the light of the new. Such a faith exists; its powerful instruments lie ready at hand. Prophetic religion now has an ally in what might be called revealed psychology—a science that lays bare the secret diseases of man's troubled soul and provides a serviceable therapy for healing them. Fused together by terrible necessity, religion and psychology now bend forward, as one, to succor stumbling humanity, to lift it up, anoint its wounds, and fill its cup to overflowing with the oil of peace.

"Religion and psychiatry reconciled?" you murmur.

The arguments for such reconciliation are impressive, comforting, and not too difficult for well-disposed persons to understand. Bending to the eyepiece of the comparison microscope, let us discover for ourselves how religion and psychology resemble, and how they differ from, each other.

Two Strategies, One Goal

The express purpose of religion is the achievement of the good life. As to the noble rightness of this purpose, there can hardly be a dispute. What *is* questioned in any debate on the good life is the means of effecting it—the strategy to be employed in mastering man's passions and impulses and evoking the dominant best in his nature. If religion has been right in its traditional methods, why does man need modern psychology? Conversely, if psychology is imperatively needed, what role is left for religion? Extremists and special pleaders warn us of the basic antagonism between these two approaches to the good life. We are told that if we wish to be "saved," we must choose either psychology or religion, but we certainly cannot choose both.

This all-or-nothing attitude toward two powerful instruments of human comfort and spiritual release is, we are beginning to suspect, totally unwarranted. The roots of this hostility flourish, of course, in the now barren soil of an outworn conception of man's relation to God. Champions of this fundamentalist view hesitate, apparently, to include religion among the lesser disciplines of human truth-seeking and mortal aspiration. Such inclusion, they fear, might stain the purity of the Divine. Religion to them is ultimately unrelated to the insights of science, philosophy, and art. God speaks directly to men in eternal and unchanging accents, and we, poor listeners, need no supplementary additions to His immutable revelation.

Equally resistant to the full impact of truth is the rapidly disappearing breed of scientists whose investigations are limited by the walls of the laboratory. To this elect group God is a myth, religion is organized superstition; man is an animal, the soul a figment, immortality a species of wishfulness. The "good life" proceeds without adoration, humility, or discoverable moral purpose.

Questing Inward

These opposing squadrons pitch their sullen tents at the extreme borders of today's Campus Martius. They glower, fulminate, hurl an occasional lance at each other. But on the broad and intensely troubled plain stretching between them, the great bulk of mankind seethes, flounders, cries out, and falls in dubious battle against daily fears and overriding uncertainties. How grateful they are for any drop of comforting truth, for any ration of spiritual succor! Bewildered, leaderless, forlorn, they truly need and gratefully hearken to such accents of truth as rise above the din of battle. It is upon such as these that the blending voices of religion and psychiatry fall with maximum benefit and hope.

This blending is not factitious or superficial; it merely happens to be something new in the world, a perfect fusion of the oldest and latest discoveries about the human soul. It is amazing how many of the oldest religious beliefs parallel the new discoveries of dynamic psychology. Prophetic religion, for example, has always stressed the identity of men with one another, has based itself upon the universality of mankind, the common brotherhood of the race. Psychology today adds its voice to religion and shows men that there really is no uniqueness in the essential human problems that confront us all. Psychology proclaims that men are basically similar in their weaknesses and strengths. Our fears and worries may assume different shapes, but stripped of all their masquerades, the fears of men are quite identical: the fear of loneliness, rejection, inferiority, unmanageable anger, illness, and death. Nor are men unique in the spiritual hunger which unites them even more than does physical hunger: the hunger for love, recognition, understanding, security, belongingness, and a satisfying

17

communion with the wider horizon of the universe—that Power greater than man, God.

Prophetic religion throughout the ages has stressed the need for forgiveness and tolerance. Dynamic psychology now supplements this insight by teaching us that we can achieve inner health only through forgiveness—the forgiveness not only of others but also of ourselves. We must cease tormenting ourselves when we do not achieve the absolute in life. We must begin to assimilate emotionally the truth that all of life is mingled failure and success, and that no man possesses a monopoly on saintliness or sin. A tolerance for the uniqueness of every human being, and a forgiveness of shortcomings—whether they be our own or those of our human comrades—these attitudes the psychological laboratory proclaim as our guarantors of serenity.

Prophetic religion has always emphasized the importance of free will—the centrality of human responsibility. Psychology demonstrates today that many men and women are so worn with inner conflict that they are chained and frozen, unable really to make up their own minds or free to choose their own scale of values. These indecisive personalities, vacillating like a pendulum between extremes, become capable of "free will" only when the inner causes of their irresponsibility are uncovered. Not until then do they become integrated enough to take responsibility for their own decisions and their own lives.

Prophetic religion has always taught the danger of rigid pride, of insincerity, the corrosive effects of cynicism and hopelessness, the need for consistency in emotion and in action. All of these insights of religion are now verified by the

Questing Inward

subtle explorations of dynamic psychology, whereby men and women are taught how to escape the emotional pitfalls of depression, arrogance, hypocrisy, and that practical atheism which is human cruelty.

Prophetic religion has proclaimed the faith that this is a world full of divine resources for change and growth and that man has within himself untapped reservoirs both of goodness and of creativity. Modern psychology echoes and illustrates this conviction of religion, and by helping men to grow and to modify their character structure it demonstrates in a new field how radiant and zestful life can become and how truly miraculous are the resources of God for human salvation—resources made available through the pioneering efforts of scientists, psychologists, therapists.

Religion has always emphasized unity—not only the unity of God but the unity of man within himself. Here, too, psychotherapy approached the religious insight and dream. Sigmund Freud, the founder of psychoanalysis, really had a spiritual purpose, even though he may not have been aware of it. For if each man is created in the image of God, and God is one—then it follows that if man allows himself to become a split soul, an inwardly warring personality, he actually denies his Divine image. The work of psychotherapy parallels the religious drive by creating in man an emotional and psychological togetherness that makes him one as God is one.

Far from being antagonistic, religion and psychiatry are mutually supplementary. Each is capable of supporting man at points where the other is weakest or has failed. There is no danger that psychiatry will displace religion, nor is it any longer possible for religion to sweep back the rising tide of psychological knowledge that is floating man off the submerged ledges of grief and perplexity. Harried mankind needs both religion and psychiatry. Men should no longer deny themselves the assistance to be derived either from the revealed word of God or the findings of "revealed psychology." Only in the mighty confluence of these two tides shall we find peace of mind.

Am I being unorthodox when I suggest that it is in the mighty confluence of dynamic psychology and prophetic religion that modern man is most likely to find peace of mind? Will I be called a revolutionary if I suggest that religion, for all its wonderful achievements, has been responsible for many morbid consciences, infinite confusions, and painful distortions in the psychic life of people? Religion to this day confuses symptoms with causes and is too easily satisfied with surface cures. Furthermore, much religion in the Western world remains on the child level. Perhaps the majority of men and women are happy with that kind of child religion because they themselves are immature. It is my belief, however, that a better society is going to require mature individuals and in order to achieve that maturity religion itself must become mature.

I am convinced, in other words, that religion, which already has made its peace with Copernicus and with Darwin, will have to make peace with Freud. Today religion, with the exception of fundamentalist sects, does not quarrel too much with modern astronomy or with modern biology. It took decades and centuries for a peace pact to be written between religion and science. Perhaps theology battled against the telescope and the microscope partly out of the inevitable vanity of our human species. It is understandable that people should cling to the comforting thought that this earth is the center of creation and that man, the divine creature, is distinguished from the beginning from all other species on earth. But the reconciliation was effected, the forward step was taken, the fusion of science and faith was achieved. Today a still more important fusion must be made. Religion must make its peace with modern psychology, not so much for the sake of harmony as for the immeasurable benefit that will accrue to the human race.

My words are not directed to those blessed souls that are quietly content in the arms of some traditional religion, nor are they intended for mystics who have found their own private way to serenity. I hope, however, that these chapters may help those disturbed and questing souls in this modern world who cannot "go home again" to old theologies or ancient psychologies, those who seek a way of life from a religion and a psychology that have grown wise enough to pool their great resources. A religion that will joyously welcome the gifts of modern psychology will be able to deal with human evil in terms of change and creation, will know the darkness of human nature but not be dismayed by it, will be neither naïve about human goodness nor pessimistic about human power. Such a religion will be able not merely to describe the good life and its great goals but also to implement that life with indispensable means. Aided by the tools of dynamic psychology, religion will be able to understand far more subtly and profoundly why men hate rather than love, why men grow afraid, surrender to morbidity, and turn in bitterness against the Power greater than man. At the same time this wiser religion will be able to show men and women how to achieve a freer conscience, a less counterfeit love, a more integrated courage, and an undistorted life-affirming communion with God.

I see now (in my mind's eye only, for the rabbinic friend of my youth has long since departed) the smile of approval on the worn lips of my old mentor as I indulge in these heresies. "God does not question [he tells me] the courses by which rivulets flow to the sea. He holds the waters of life in his hand, and sees the predestined path that each pilgrim soul must follow in its quest for salvation. Sects and orthodoxies perish, but timelessly, indestructibly, man's journey toward the peace of God goes irrevocably on."

CHAPTER TWO

Conscience Doth Make Cowards...

It was Montaigne, that not-so-hard-bitten French skeptic, who declared, "Man is an amoral creature inevitably committed to the moral enterprise." For man, predatory and unregenerate though he is, cannot live without certain ideals; he is driven by some inexorable necessity to seek goodness as well as truth. This is the way man is made. It is as much his nature to be aware of good *and* evil as it is the nature of a tree to bear fruit.

Mankind would never have developed standards and ideals if these germinating forces were not latent within the very plasm of humanity. Even though prophets and saints berated man for his failings, they long ago understood that he is equipped with a "still small voice" just as truly as he is equipped with hands and feet. Man's capacity to feel guilt when he fails to live up to the moral code demonstrates that he is a creature of conscience and spirit.

The philosopher Kant once declared that nothing proved to him the greatness of God more convincingly than the starry heavens and the moral conscience within us. To which Freud ironically adds: "The stars are unquestionably superb, but where the conscience is concerned, God has been guilty of an uneven and careless piece of work." For it is undeniably true that the same marvelous faculty that guides us along the road to morality often acts as a sadistic slave driver, a self-accusing fury, and a tireless jobber in guilt. The damage wrought by these aspects of conscience is incalculable. Much of our mental and physical illness—a whole host of fears, anxieties, and hatreds—springs from the seeds of false conscience that man has somehow contrived to sow during his life.

There is, of course, a *true* conscience, which has nothing to do with self-hatred or a false emphasis on one's own unworthiness. This genuine conscience, Erich Fromm declares, "forms a part of integrated personality, and the following of its demands is an affirmation of the whole self." This form of conscience is the sterling mark of maturity; we see it in the inflexible standards that the artist, doctor, and teacher set for themselves; it is present in every father and mother who rear their children with love and devotion. We hear deep chords of true conscience in the voices of those who—like Roosevelt or Lincoln—champion the poor or redeem the afflicted. These are the noblest affirmations of man's love for his fellows—the very voice of God speaking through His creatures.

Unfortunately, however, the voice of conscience does not always take this high, healthful form of expression. Oftener than not, it follows the line of Paul, Augustine, Calvin, and Luther—all of whom were obsessed by the notion of man's wickedness. Their cry is the cry of most Western religions: "Atone, you miserable human worm! Smite yourself with the rod of self-punishment. Lacerate your guilty soul with the knout of Conscience, else ye be not worthy of the sight of God."

Religion (not God) is to blame for this morbid, guilt-ridden

Conscience Doth Make Cowards

attitude. It must be admitted, however, that religion has a few extenuating circumstances on its side. In the very process of creating man's conscience, it was essential to introduce concepts of guilt and sin—valuable and necessary in restraining man's primitive instinctual drives toward murder, incest, and cannibalism. These taboos became the beacon "shalt-nots" that guided men into the first safe harbors of human culture. The whole fascinating story runs something like this:

When religion was born, man was just emerging from barbarian infancy. The primary needs were the acquisition of the high ideals of monogamy, family fidelity, brotherly compassion, and social righteousness in a world still incapable of distinguishing clearly between right and wrong. The harsh underscoring of the contrast between good and evil was justified; before our evil instincts could be tamed and harnessed to serve our good instincts, rigid demarcations had to be established. Before undertaking the tremendous task of pervading the whole of human life, religion had to gain a firm beachhead on the shores of man's unregenerate soul.

Freud discovered that what was true for the *early stages of mankind* also holds true for the early stages in the development of *each individual*. As children, we do not clearly distinguish between good and evil, or even between fantasy and fact. Our fathers and mothers must curb our rebellious instincts, force the distasteful medicine of authority down our unwilling throats. Freedom, self-reliance, independence are postponed for the sake of our own physical growth and expanding spirits. In the stages of human development from infancy to adolescence, it is quite proper for religion to present rules of moral behavior as categorical commandments. It is

Peace of Mind

through such prohibitions and permissions that a conscience is woven on the life loom of the growing personality.

Too often, however, the shelters of childhood become the prisons of maturity; dependent reliance upon others becomes weak indecisiveness, and many of us are tragically afraid to liberate ourselves from the chains of yesteryear. A false idea of religion still encourages that fear and hardens those chains; it helps keep men and women in subjection to their childish and adolescent conscience at a time when they should be trusted to make a proper distinction between fantasy and fact, dream and deed.

Religious teachers throughout the ages have seldom distinguished wisely between an immoral thought and an immoral act. Rather have they maintained that a lustful, envious, or destructive thought is quite as evil as a lustful, envious, or destructive deed. Christianity, profoundly influenced by the doctrine that desire is equivalent to the commission of sin (Christ, in effect, maintains that a man who lusts in his heart commits adultery), advises man to choke down every evil thought, lest he fall into the pit of eternal damnation.

The overall strategy employed by religion in the struggle against evil can be defined in one word: *repression*. With few exceptions Western religion has insisted that men and women can become good only through the stern repression of sensual thoughts and impulses. And this mechanism of repression by which we mute the horrid voice of "sin" is responsible for much of the grief, illness, and anxiety that lash the soul of modern man.

Clearly, the "choke-it-down" formula has tragically failed to secure the good life for mankind. Gross and pitiful evi-

Conscience Doth Make Cowards

dences of this failure encumber our private lives, clog our social progress. The spread of mental illness throughout the Western world, the prevalent mood of insecurity, marital conflict, personal depression, not to mention wars and mass murders, should indicate the inadequacy of the classic religious approach to the problem of evil. The technique of repression —the tight-lipped denial of all our hostile and sensual thoughts as the prerequisite to happy living—*simply has not worked!*

The truth is, of course, that all of us have amoral fantasies and unmoral dreams. They are part of our mortal equipment. To deny their existence is impossible; to bury these thoughts and fantasies in the subcellar of our minds is to invite explosions of guilt, aggression, and even physical pain!

Dynamic psychology proves that if the evil is driven out of the light of consciousness, it merely goes underground. The reality of childish shame or rage is not exterminated by disavowal; it is merely locked up—potential dynamite in a hidden storeroom of our psyche. Outraged by tyrannical repression, our unconventional or unacceptable impulses outwit us by disguising themselves in new forms. They become our worst inner enemies, assaulting our nerves, laying siege to our peace of mind, tormenting us with a sense of failure, making us feel depressed and inferior, driving us from excess to excess against our will. We develop high blood pressure or stomach ulcers (Dr. Alvarez of the Mayo Clinic has called the stomach ulcer the "wound-stripe of civilization"). Men and women who, influenced by traditional religion, try to uproot every vagrant desire from their minds sometimes transform themselves into self-torturing masochists or intolerant fanatics. Many so-called "good" people are moral hypocrites who compensate for the enormous "inner lie" of their lives by displaying subtle cruelties to their mates, children, or society.

Total repression of primitive impulses is not only impossible; it is highly undesirable. For the happy fact is that the energy inherent in our passionate impulses can be diverted into socially useful channels. This process, called sublimation, is the profoundest spiritualizing factor in man's life. Many of our most valuable social and intellectual activities draw their energy from sources originally libidinous. The surgeon's skill sometimes is a splendid example of the sublimation of an early childhood urge to cut. Neither to deny the existence of our basic energies nor to unbridle them in acts of raw license is the duty of man. We should acknowledge without shame the instinctual sources of our energy, then strive to translate this energy into the almost divine forms of art, science, beauty, goodness, and happiness.

Religion too frequently has encouraged men to make a complete detour of their unangelic nature. But dynamic psychology encourages men to bring the dark and uncomfortable aspects of their inner life to the surface. It has too many magnificent successes to its credit in hundreds of clinics and laboratories for us to discount its validity. Its tested method is to enable men and women to "talk out" their innermost thoughts, and by that "token release" to render harmless most of the explosive time bombs which have been buried in the ground of their psyches.

By carefully distinguishing between thought and deed, by laying bare the elemental nature of our impulses and their role in our psychic economy, psychotherapy has been able to evolve a reassuring approach to the problem of evil. The

Conscience Doth Make Cowards

amazing good news from this quarter is that men can best conquer their antisocial impulses not by denying or repressing them, *but by acknowledging and facing them!*

Verbal expression of these deeply repressed impulses actually does lead to a diminution of the urge to action. Although it may appear strange and paradoxical at first, it has been established that when normal men and women learn how to express in words their deep-lying desires and rages, their destructive and immoral compulsions become controllable. Divested of fear and anxiety, released men and women leave the doctor's chamber, free to pour their energy into channels of health and creative happiness.

Physical ills, as well as psychic ailments, sometimes miraculously disappear. The psychiatrist may take a man suffering from some common physical disturbance such as hypertension, ulcer, or asthma, and gradually encourage him to talk out his inner anxieties, conflicts, angers, and desires. The patient learns that he can express in words his most antisocial thoughts without fear that antisocial action will result from this verbal release.

Certainly, this method is diametrically opposed to the traditional procedure of religion. Instead of outlawing our evil thoughts, we are encouraged to acknowledge them in fantasy and thought, thereby permitting the conscious part of our ego to face them in full light, to disarm them, to triumph over them, and even to put their energies to a constructive use.

Psychoanalysis and Confessional

"But," you ask, "does not the confessional also encourage

'talking out' one's innermost thoughts?" What is the difference between the confession of one's sins to a priest or a rabbi and the expression of anxiety to a psychoanalyst? There are many differences both in form and in content. Let me say at the very outset that there are some enlightened priests who, having absorbed many of the newer truths that come from the realm of psychiatric exploration, can and do make the confessional occasions for real help. Likewise, pastors and rabbis, as they inform themselves about the new laws of interpersonal relationships and human motivation, can make religious counseling a source of enormous aid to confused and tormented human beings. However, it is true that though religious confession lifts many burdens from the conscience, the process is usually too much on the surface, and it is seldom that deep insight or permanent character change is effected by this process. Atonement, rather than growth, is the aim of the religious confessional, whereas psychotherapy does not require that you feel sorry for your sins so long as you *outgrow* them!

Confession by its very nature serves to reinforce inner guilt feelings. The sinner comes to the clergyman as the child to its father, seeking forgiveness and expecting punishment. He has already learned through experience what coins of penance he must pay for various degrees of sin, and there is little inner growth experienced in this well-worn routine of confession and ecclesiastical reproof. The confessional touches only the surface of a man's life. Nor does the confessor usually attempt to probe behind the penitent's façade of rationalization. While a certain amount of incidental release may be obtained through the confessional, the character structure of the peni-

Conscience Doth Make Cowards

tent is not altered, nor are the psychogenic roots of his "sin" laid bare.

Let me illustrate by an example. A deeply troubled man, thirty-five, married, humbly discloses to his religious counselor that he is carrying on an extramarital affair. He is very conscious of the pain that he is inflicting on his wife and family. He knows he is doing wrong. The clergyman warns him that adultery is an ugly sin in the sight of God and man, and urges him to bring the affair to a close. The penitent promises to do so, but after a sharp struggle falls back into his old adulterous practice. The advice fails because the spiritual advisor has thrown no light on the *causes* of this man's sorry plight. He is urged to display more "will power" and "stay away" from the other woman. Every minister knows how often these are ineffective counsels.

Humorously commenting on a similar situation, Sigmund Freud tells the story of a country bumpkin visiting a hotel for the first time. Preparing for bed, the countryman attempts to blow out the electric light as though it were a candle. He blows powerfully, but of course the bulb is not extinguished. Not until he learns to snap off the switch in the corner of the room will the light go off. So it is often with an adulterer. Not all the will power in the world will enable him to extinguish the cause of his unfortunate behavior. He must be shown *where the switch is* before he can control the powerful current being generated in his unconscious life.

Psychology, unlike the confessional, seeks out the breeding ground that is generating its spew of trouble. In the case of the unfaithful husband, it eradicates the neurotic source of the difficulty, alters the direction of the undesirable drives, and

31

quite literally changes a person from an infantile weakling into a mature adult. Analysis reveals to him the underlying causes of his neurotic behavior, traces them far back to their childish origins. It shows him where the "switch" is, and teaches him how to cut the undesirable current out of his life.

All this is achieved without generating a "guilty conscience" in the person seeking help. He also discovers that the talking out of his inner drives and anxieties does not involve him in any punishment at the hands of the physician. He is free to speak without being judged. To his amazement he encounters neither approval nor disapproval, but a detached, calm, healing understanding. He is not told what to do or how to act, but is strengthened in his capacity to face himself with honesty and make his own independent decisions. As he expresses his angers, resentments, passion, lusts, and envies, he begins to see them in perspective. He realizes how absurd and out of place many of these long-repressed impulses are in the total emotional economy of his adult life. He comes to understand their origin in the turmoil of his childhood and their meaninglessness in the larger framework of his present values, and he freely rejects them in the creative light of his newly won understanding.

These, then, are some of the differences between religious confession and psychological verbalization. A man who depends upon a religious seer or guide to tell him what is right and wrong will, oftener than not, live his life in the shadow of uncomfortable guilt and unresolved anxieties. Furthermore, he will always be in danger of possessing only a derived conscience borrowed continually from the priest or pastor. His "still small voice" will consist of other men's commands and prohibitions. He will always be dependent—a moral slave to some external code.

The man who has "lived through" intense psychotherapeutic experience has learned many lessons about his own inner nature but among the most valuable is this—*self-understanding rather than self-condemnation is the way to inner peace and mature conscience.* Through looking fearlessly at all of his nature, he comes to see what actions are compatible with adult fulfillment. He faces ghosts of childhood and adolescence—ghosts which he had locked in unremembered chambers of the past—and as he faces them, they vanish. The frightening thoughts, the horrible fantasies, the guilt-laden dreams—thrown by speech upon the screen of consciousness —become controllable. He learns to say himself, "Here is that hateful thought again, that sensual yearning, that self-deprecating tendency. I know you all and I am no longer afraid of you because I see your true size. As long as I locked you within the prison cell of repression you seemed like giants to me, but now I realize that you are only puny, misshapen dwarfs. You can no longer compel me to commit cruel or immoral deeds that will hurt myself or those whom I love. You now are in the light, you bogeymen of the past, and in the light you have lost all tyrannical power over me."

This process of liberation can be illustrated by an analogy from a common experience. A man in his youth falls in love with a beautiful young girl. Fate separates them and the man keeps his dream image alive in memory, refusing all the happiness that life could give him in the sure conviction that when he lost his youthful love he lost everything. After many years he meets a shrew with a shrill voice and a face furrowed with lines of petulance and pettiness. To his amazement it is his lost love. He learns that many of the ideal virtues he had found in her were actually of his own creation. He sees what he has escaped. He realizes how wrong he has been to spend his years in emotional servitude to a vision of youth. Face to face with the reality of the woman whom he had loved and lost, he finds the strength to liberate himself from the shackles of memory. Now that he has seen her stripped of all the idealizing veils of memory, he finds that he is able to laugh at himself; he is free of haunting pain. Those moments of revelation have taken away the power of the past over him.

Too frequently, our conscience turns out to be a harsh-voiced shrew, unworthy of our love.

The Masks of Conscience

Many are the guises in which conscience revenges itself upon us. It is a masked tormentor quite capable of inflicting illness, insanity, even suicide, upon its victim. The deep findings of psychiatry reveal that suicide, for example, may be an atonement that guilty conscience imposes on the self-killer. He wishes to expiate his "crime"—usually some infantile peccadillo—and does so upon the altar of his own body.

Psychosomatic medicine, one of the striking new achievements of science, is proving that multitudes of fine men and women are unwittingly destroying themselves because they have never learned to know and accept themselves with all of the crude, elemental drives and impulses that are common to human nature. I think now of a splendid young man who literally was choked to death by asthma, because after his

Conscience Doth Make Cowards

mother's death he married a girl that his mother had not liked. His extreme sense of guilt not only prevented him from enjoying the fullness of married life with a beautiful woman, but actually caused a five-year illness and ultimate death.

Clearly, a more tolerant conscience pattern, which is not fixated on an immature level of right and wrong, is essential for the inner peace of normal adults. Religion must now recognize that our deep antisocial impulses when denied and repressed do not disappear miraculously from reality; the more we treat them like criminals, the more vengeance they take against us. Adults who strive for total repression of their impulses in the realm of imagination wreak havoc either on their bodies or their spirits.

The religion of the future should take a page from the notebook of the psychotherapist, encouraging men to tolerate their unacceptable impulses, to sublimate them, and at the same time to discipline themselves to a finer and more generous program of action. It must strengthen mature men and women to realize that everyone has desires and fantasies antisocial in nature. Only when their presence is acknowledged rather than repressed can they be prevented from exercising dominion over us in the vital realm of action.

Furthermore, normal men and women do possess trustworthy consciences, whether they know it or not. It is an encouraging fact that God has given us a special manifestation of His Divinity in the healthy human conscience which holds the earth like a spinning gyroscope on its course. For in spite of all temptations to swing off our orbit into eccentric or erratic courses, most of us do develop a discriminating, serviceable, and non-neurotic sense of right and wrong. And it is precisely this well-adjusted, enduring conscience that creates a magnetic field of serenity in our own lives and in the lives of those around us.

We must learn to trust our own conscience just as we learn to trust our own eyes, nerves, and digestion. A well-known Harvard psychiatrist tells of a young woman who developed grave fears lest she actually commit evil deeds bordering on murder which came to her in thought. Investigation showed that she had been heavily dependent on her husband, who was then away at war. She had leaned too heavily on his code of conduct to safeguard her—and now that these safeguards were withdrawn, she developed an abnormal fear that she would be victimized by her evil inclinations. The doctor was able to show her that she, like all normal people, really possessed a perfectly reasonable, excellent set of standards of her own, though she had never dared to use them. Her plight was as absurd as that of a person who dared not walk lest his muscles fail to support him. We shall do well to realize that both our muscles and our consciences grow within us without our volition or knowledge, and we can rely on both of them.

Concerning the operations of conscience, religion must learn from psychiatry what the medical men of our armed forces have learned about the treatment of battle fatigue and wartime neuroses. This war has produced some miraculous cures merely by making possible, through various psychiatric techniques, the verbal expression of fears, guilt, and anxiety— the three elements that go to make up conscience. The "token release" of speech thus achieved has saved thousands of our soldiers and sailors who were physical and mental wrecks. As one grateful and very intelligent corporal remarked: "Ex-

Conscience Doth Make Cowards

pressing my fears—putting them into words—made them evaporate harmlessly like steam escaping from a kettle."

Seal up even a small teakettle, place it over a flame, and it will wreck a house. But let the powerful vapors escape, and the kettle *sings!*

I do not suggest that everyone should be running constantly to a psychologist for assistance. The specters of conscience can often be dispelled by a reassuring conversation with a friend, brother, or partner. For it is a great human truth that when we unlock our hearts to any sympathetic listener, our burdens often take wings. And in the process we make a remarkable discovery. We find that the other person also is possessed at times by angry thoughts or sensual moods and this very discovery of mutuality of experience results in mutuality of liberation.

Theoretically, religion wishes to make men serene and inwardly peaceful by teaching a loving and forgiving God. But in practice, there is too much undissolved wrath and punishment in most religions. Conscience, abetted by this kind of punitive religion, doth indeed make cowards of us all, by keeping us in the posture of the boy who fears the woodshed ministrations of an angry father. We must lay aside all such fears, and view ourselves neither as naughty children nor as spotless angels, but as mature men and women with all our mortal imperfections on our heads.

"There is a crack in everything that God has made," says Emerson. The thought gives us a comforting humility. Somehow, it prompts us to believe that God hears no sweeter music than the cracked chimes of the courageous human spirit ringing in imperfect acknowledgment of His perfect love.

37

CHAPTER THREE

Love Thyself Properly

I T is a striking irony that while religion is often quite analytical and subtle in its understanding of a man's obligations to others, it is quaintly naïve about his obligation to himself. It assumes that men need to be taught in detail exactly how they should act to one another, but these same men are supposed to be innately wise or spontaneously intelligent about the way they should treat themselves. Herein lies one of the supreme fallacies of religion and ethics.

The fact is that men have to be taught the immorality of tragic self-hate, just as they have to be taught the immorality of cruelty and callousness to others.

Love and hate are emotions which attach themselves at times to other persons and at times to ourselves. It is one of the great discoveries of modern psychology that our attitudes toward ourselves are just as complicated as our attitudes toward others—sometimes more so. The great commandment of religion, "Thou shalt love thy neighbor as thyself," might now be better interpreted to mean, "Thou shalt love thyself properly, and *then* thou wilt love thy neighbor."

A story is told of a prominent social worker who received a letter from a society woman who wanted to join in his crusade

Love Thyself Properly

to help the poor children of New York. The society woman spoke at some length of her imperfections and ended by saying that perhaps her zeal for *his* cause would make up for her shortcomings. He wrote a brief reply: "Dear Madam, Your truly magnificent shortcomings at present are too great. Nothing could prevent you from visiting them on victims of your humility. I advise that you love yourself more before you squander any love on others."

Many authorities in the fields of ethics and religion will grow indignant with this view. "You are proclaiming a very dangerous doctrine," they will say. "By advising men to love themselves you are merely sanctioning an intensified selfishness. Human beings love themselves too much already. What people must be taught is that self-love is evil, that it must be conquered, and that the true goal of life is the rejection of self in the altruistic service of others."

This condemnation of selfishness and exaltation of altruism is the traditional attitude of religion. It holds up a worthy goal to be sure, but there are many errors in its estimate of human nature. Is it *true* that we are spontaneously good to ourselves? The evidence points in quite the opposite direction. Men may *wish* to be good to themselves, but how misguided and unwise they are in their attempts to reach that goal! The fact is that we often treat ourselves more rigidly, more fanatically, more vengefully, than we do others. Suicide, self-mutilation, and more subtle forms of self-degradation such as alcoholism, drug addiction, and promiscuity are pitiful proofs of this. Such self-hate is not restricted to the weak and the insane. No less a man than John Jay Chapman, the distinguished American essayist, was guilty of violent self-hate. After a quarrel with a casual acquaintance he thrust his hand into a blazing fire, burning it so severely that it had to be amputated. Van Gogh, the artist, chopped off his own ear for a similar reason. A well-known editor threw himself into a tub of boiling water to atone for a debauch. These are extreme cases, but violent forms of aggression against the self occur daily and less dramatically in the lives of ordinary men and women.

Such actions constitute a crime not only against ourselves but against society. He who hates himself, who does not have proper regard for his own capacities, powers, compassions, actually can have no respect for others. Deep within himself he will hate his brothers when he sees in them his own marred image. Love for oneself is the foundation of a brotherly society and personal peace of mind. By loving oneself I do not mean coddling oneself, indulging in vanity, conceit, self-glorification. I do, however, insist on the necessity of a proper self-regard as a prerequisite of the good and the moral life. "A man must associate in friendly reverence for himself." In a deep sense we must have good domestic relations with ourselves before we can have good foreign relations with others.

Psychology today can help us understand that one of the reasons we have failed to find peace of mind is that we have not yet learned *how* to be good to ourselves and, therefore, have not yet learned how to be good to others. Psychology reveals the underlying causes of false self-love and destructive self-hatred. Religion, allied with psychology, can demonstrate just what true self-regard means.

Theoretically, religion has always been concerned with the achievement of true self-love. It eternally proclaims the value of every human personality, the sanctity of every man. But it

Love Thyself Properly

has been strangely impotent to implement that sanctity. We know that our mental hospitals are filled with extremists who mutilate themselves physically. But all the streets of the world are teeming with men and women who mutilate themselves spiritually and mentally in the invisible ways of self-criticism and self-degradation. It is indeed time for us to study examples of false attitudes to the self, and to learn what psychology has discovered about the changing, contradictory evolution of the human personality.

Development of Self

The story of the human self and its development is as fascinating as any romance. It is a story filled with heroes and villains and adventures, of daring and defeat. The road this self must travel to reach maturity and peace is lined with dangers, obstacles, and misconceptions. The greatest of these misconceptions is the notion that the self is a kind of substance implanted in men at birth, and that its characteristics are preformed and unchanging.

How terribly untrue!

The human self is not a gift; it is an achievement. It is not a static reality, sprung full-blown from the head of God. Rather it is a painfully earned progress past lions in the way —a triumph over ogres real and imaginary. The attainment of a self is a running battle, a continuing process, and a victory that is never fully consummated until the chambers of our heart flutter and fill for the last time.

At the beginning of the "saga of self" we face a booming, buzzing confusion. Our eyes awake to blurred lights and in-

41

distinct shapes. We hear soft voices which soothe us or loud noises which terrify us, and as we gradually adjust ourselves to the rocking, uncertain earth, our restless minds begin to make a little pattern of order here, a little design of meaning there. Our emotions are without armor, defenseless and tender, and we feel the tensions that crackle like lightning through the atmosphere of the grown-up world. Gradually we adjust to the strange kingdom of childhood, but there are always dangers lurking in shaded corners, strange gusts of emotion that sweep through us like cold winds on an open prairie. Emotions of jealous possessiveness seize us when rivals threaten our primacy in the realm of our parents' love, new brothers and sisters awaken slumbering giants of jealousy and envy. Fear and anger, insecurity and pain, blot out the sun of many a growing day.

As soon as we become masters of this little island of our earliest childhood, we find ourselves driven forth to a new and stranger world called "school," which fascinates and frightens us at the same time. Rivalry with our fellows, the awkward testing of our strength, the trials of puberty, the little failures and great losses which mar the beauty of adolescence, tempt us to refuse the mixed blessings of growth. We yearn to regress to some earlier level, some older form of behavior where we were infinitely more shielded and protected.

The adolescent at moments wants to return to that well-loved country of his childhood where there was less competition, where everything was given to him. Every new stage of life is a shattering one emotionally and forces us to build some new adjustment out of broken fragments of our past, out of the precious shards of earlier molds.

Love Thyself Properly

Gradually, if we become well-adjusted adults we learn how to accept the loss of our earlier privileges. We face the competition of our contemporaries and learn to share without too much bitterness our gifts and selves with others. We can stand punishment and immediate frustration without undue anxiety. We realize that for us the way lies ahead, and that it is too late to turn back, that such a retreat will cause only unhappiness.

Some, however, do not survive the pitfalls along the road to maturity. Many never escape the childish or the adolescent, and remain "fixated" at an immature level of self-development. Family discord, a broken home, rejection by a parent, or discrimination because of a physical handicap may deflect the growing ego, and instead of a wise love of self we have a sick, morbid rejection of self. This may lead to narcissism—a perverted form of self-adoration mixed with and growing out of self-contempt.

A common example will illustrate this point. A small boy desperately in need of affection from his parents finds himself frustrated in his yearning. His parents hate one another and resent the burden of the child who stands in the path of their freedom. Rejected by them, and believing deeply therefore in his own worthlessness, he compensates by diverting all of his own capacity for affection onto himself, and is forced into the position of morbidly loving himself as he would like his parents to love him. Such a boy becomes a "Citizen Kane," unable truly to give or accept love, imprisoned within the barren walls of his self-absorption. Such narcissism is not a healthy variety of self-love, but is an inferiority feeling born of rejection and wearing a mask.

43

Peace of Mind

In his recent book *Rebel Without a Cause,* **Dr. Robert Lindner** studies the background of a twenty-three-year-old criminal, tracing the roots of the boy's tendencies back to childhood. He found that the boy's father was excessively sadistic, and that the boy's mother was insufficient protection against the father. The boy grew up to feel that nobody in the world had any real feeling for him, and that the only way he could obtain any good from this unwilling world was to wrench it away at the point of a gun. He saw himself as isolated, alone in a hostile environment, all others as strangers and enemies. Under the loving care of the doctor he was at last able to renounce such narcissism and become a useful outgoing citizen of the world who could give and take without fear.

Some narcissists literally love themselves to death. They suffocate in the closed room in which all windows have been transformed into mirrors. Stephen Vincent Benét, in *John Brown's Body,* gives an unforgettable picture of the tragic narcissist in his portrayal of Lucy, the Southern belle who has been so fixated upon the level of morbid self-love that she is repelled by the thought of marriage and the possibility that anybody else might possess her body. Standing in front of her mirror she addresses her own image in these revealing words:

> *"Honey, I love you," she whispered.*
> *"I love you, honey.*
> *Nobody loves you like I do, do they, sugar?*
> *Nobody knows but Lucy how sweet you are.*
> *You mustn't get married, honey. You*
> *mustn't leave me.*

Love Thyself Properly

We'll always be pretty and sweet to all of them,
won't we, honey?

We'll always have beaus to dance with and
tunes to dance to,
But you mustn't leave me, honey. I
couldn't bear it.
You mustn't leave me for any man."

Narcissism of this sort may possibly look like self-love, but it is a bogus emotion. It is self-absorption without self-respect. "Citizen Kane" and Benét's "Lucy" are both cases of arrested development—characters who are never really fond or sure of themselves—Citizen Kane because he seeks always to compensate himself for his deep-seated conviction of his own worthlessness, and Lucy because she has projected an imaginary picture of a lovable self which she dare not surrender to grasp reality. The narcissist, as Dr. Schilder points out in *Goals and Desires of Man,* is always distorted in his social relations. He looks upon others merely as bestowers of love and admiration. He is never satisfied with himself until he receives applause from others.

This excessive self-centeredness often takes punitive forms. Egocentric energy, finding outlet in daydreams of self-glorification, is withdrawn from normal pursuits and external love objects; frequently professional failure and abject misery result. It is as though the sufferer had a psychic tapeworm which incessantly demanded the food of love and approval in ever-increasing portions. *He is starving for a type and quantity of sustenance which no mature individual can reasonably expect!* This infantilism leads to broken marriages, inability to

45

get along with one's associates in business or society, and even strangles that strongest of emotions—parental love.

There are many temptations to self-contempt and self-destruction along the route that the ego takes to maturity. As a matter of fact, one reason why man can be more continuously cruel to himself than to anyone else is that he is always available to himself as an object of attack. Other people are intermittently present as objects of our aggression, but our own ego is always there, even in sleep, as a citadel to be stormed, a fortress to be smashed, an enemy to be destroyed. Suicide is only the extreme proof of the fact that man does not necessarily love himself. Many people go throughout life committing partial suicide—destroying their talents, energies, creative qualities. Indeed, to learn how to be good to oneself is often more difficult than to learn how to be good to others.

A great tragedy of the past twenty years was the partial suicide through misinterpretation-of-self of F. Scott Fitzgerald, one of America's finest writers. A man whose talent was so plain, whose way was so clear, should have had nothing but richness and joy. But he was so tortured by misgivings and self-doubts of an irrational nature that some of the best years of his life remained fruitless, barren, racked with self-loathing.

Inferiority Complex May Hide Self-Hate

There are myriad ways in which we show contempt and cruelty rather than respect and kindness to ourselves. Feelings of inferiority are among the commonest symptoms of self-hate. How often we attribute to our neighbors abilities and powers which they do not possess! We feel inferior to them,

Love Thyself Properly

and an infinite amount of tragedy comes from this form of self-deprecation and inner self-contempt. We yearn to be like these others; to buy the same clothes, the same furniture; to speak and act as they do. Our exaggerated idea of their abilities is a weapon against ourselves as we sink into orgies of self-criticism and flagellate ourselves before the altar of someone else's personality. The fallacy here is that we tend to see ourselves as an imperfectly evolving "process" freighted with old shortcomings and inadequacies—while our neighbors are seen as finished products, surfaced at least with the lacquer of assurance and poise. If we could but realize all men and women bear within themselves the scars of many a lost battle, we would judge our own lacerated skins less harshly.

We meet examples of this self-underestimation every day. Commonest of all is the girl who feels that her inferiority is so great that she will always be completely "unworthy of a good man." Consequently, she quarrels with every eligible suitor and contrives to destroy the very qualities that make her eminently worthy and capable of a successful marriage. Other examples abound: the man in business who is afraid to expand and grasp normal opportunities because he is convinced of his inevitable failure; the professional man always certain that his abilities and ideas are inferior compared with those of his colleagues; the brilliant youth terrified of his college examination; the charming woman disparaging her social capabilities when measured by the yardstick of her neighbors —all these fine human beings, inwardly hating themselves, are really "hanging judges" conducting their own private inquisitions and condemning many wonderful talents to dangle from the scaffold of their insecurity.

Peace of Mind

To one who goes through life hypnotized by these thoughts of inferiority, we say: "The amazing paradox is that no one sees you as you see yourself. In actuality, you are quite strong and wise and successful. You have done rather well in making a tolerable human existence out of the raw materials at your disposal. You have a home, a business, a reputation. There are those who love and honor you for what you really are. Is it not tragic, then, that you alone are looking at yourself through dark-tinted glasses? Your private information is incorrect. Take off your dark-colored glasses, assume your place as a peer in the adult world, and realize that your strength is adequate to meet the problems of that world. You are better, more capable, more successful, more creative than you imagine!"

These dark and muddy anxieties and distorted attitudes to self arise in a number of ways. Suppose, for example, that a child has lost his father through death. Instead of the death being wisely explained, the child is left with a feeling of mystery and comes to the conclusion that he has been deserted. His father, he thinks, has run away. That boy becomes a man who unconsciously goes through life always afraid of being rejected by friends, employers, or society. Proper self-regard is lost to him because of an adult folly long ago. The boy did not understand that his father did not willingly leave him; yet in his mind the childish thought forever remained that his parent did not love him and therefore deserted him.

If we are subtle enough, we can find many other sources of human self-distortion. Here is a person who was made to feel as a child that he was loved or treasured conditionally; that only if he lived up to his parents' expectations could he justify himself. The cold tycoon, the ruthless industrialist, may be the

Love Thyself Properly

result, always seeking more power to offset his deep feelings of insecurity. Or take the woman who from infancy has been encouraged to feel helpless and dependent and was never taught self-reliance. Her life is miserable because she is constantly searching from one marriage to another for some magic helper, some omnipotent parent, some daily miracle.

Don Juan, popularly regarded by those who do not look closely as the archetype of the great lover, was, at heart, a man who never gave or received love. His countless conquests were an attempt to disguise from himself the fact that he could not love, or even *believe* that he could be loved. His life was both a flight and a search—a search for outgoing love, and a flight from the knowledge that he didn't really believe it existed.

It is important that all of us become wise enough to recognize where we go astray in our attitudes toward ourselves and how we become enslaved to false notions of what we are and what we ought to be. Some of us think we are loving ourselves when we are really strangling or suffocating ourselves with morbid self-concern. We maintain a cruel contempt for our own capabilities and virtues or become unconscious victims of a paralyzing egocentricity. When we free ourselves from that false self-love which is narcissism, that destructive self-hatred which is masochism, we become for the first time integrated enough to become friendly with ourselves and with others. We are on the road to proper self-love. Such self-love implies many things, but above everything else it is rooted in self-respect. And no man or woman can have self-respect unless he has learned the art of renunciation and the equally vital art of self-acceptance.

Peace of Mind

Renunciation of Immaturity

Every person who wishes to attain peace of mind must learn the art of renouncing many things in order to possess other things more securely and fully. This is a most important and difficult step. As children we lived on a pleasure level. Our wishes were sovereign. When we cried, we were promptly fed; when frightened, we were consoled and protected; when sick, we were tended and healed. We had only to wail, and the adult world, concerned with our comfort, hastened to soothe and obey us. As children, we knew very little about the necessity of renunciation. The young mind simply has no experience in the postponement of satisfaction. Yet as we grow older we learn that every stage of human development calls upon us to weigh differing goods in the scales and to sacrifice some for the sake of others.

Santayana made one of his most brilliant observations when he pointed out that the great difficulty in life does not so much arise in the choice between good and evil as in the choice between good and good. For example: a man may wish to expend his organizing creative abilities in becoming a great Shakespearean actor or a powerful pulpit preacher. Obviously, he cannot be both. In early life, however, we do not realize that one desire can be quite inconsistent with another and that we must, therefore, learn to choose between desires.

The young boy may vacillate between a dozen different professions and entertain all of them in imagination and fantasy as possibilities for the future. The man who wishes to achieve stature in the mature world will have to renounce many careers in order to fulfill one. The same truth exists in the realm

Love Thyself Properly

of emotions. It is fitting and proper for the adolescent to transfer his love interest from one object of affection to another, but it is tragic in our monogamous society when the grown man still plays the role of the adolescent and sacrifices himself and his family upon the altar of his unstable feelings and daydreams.

Time is an irreversible arrow, and we can never return to the self that we sloughed off in childhood or adolescence. The man trying to wear youth's carefree clothing, the woman costuming her emotions in doll's dresses—these are pathetic figures who want to reverse time's arrow. They have not yet learned to renounce the desires that once were appropriate for an earlier level of being but are utterly out of place in succeeding chapters. Human existence means the closing of doors, *many* doors, before one great door can be opened—the door of mature love and of adult achievement.

No person can attain genuine self-respect until he achieves the knowledge of the consistent and the inconsistent. As an adult he must accept duties and responsibilities and cultivate his true fulfillment in the acre he has chosen—the acre of love and marriage, vocation, and avocation. He must be able not only to say, but to *realize* deeply within himself, that he is no longer an uninvolved free human atom. "Everything that I do," such a man must say, "is like the pebble thrown into a pool, making larger and larger ripples in the waters of other lives."

Renunciation is often painful, and we cling stubbornly to the romantic cloak-and-dagger characters of our fantasy life. Well, no one is harmed if in the safe retreat of the daydream we parade ourselves as the conquering lover, the great hero, the famous scientist we once hoped we would become. But dangerous and vain is the attempt to relive in actuality the fantasies of childhood, or to attempt to breach those barriers between the possible and the impossible which maturing years have erected.

Finally, we must renounce undue possessiveness in relation to our children, our friends—yes, even our loves. We must be big enough, in the words of Carl Sandburg, "To loosen your hands, let go and say good-by." And such renunciations must not be made merely with the lips. We must utter a ringing heart-deep "no" to our impossible desires and unattainable ambitions, and firmly recognize what this renunciation means and requires of ourselves.

It should be noted that there is a difference between renunciation and repression. A person who represses all his ambitions and wishes and denies any reality to them is on the road to misery. The person, on the other hand, who consciously renounces unrealizable and unworthy desires has strengthened himself by daring to face his life as it is and making clear to himself why he has chosen that course of action. A man who can say to himself, "I know that there is still something of the adolescent within me, and yet I know that I can ruin my life and the lives of others if I should smash the mature pattern which I now possess; therefore, for the sake of abiding and permanent happiness, I willingly sacrifice the ephemeral temptation"—such a man has achieved the wisdom of renunciation without repression.

We shall become free of inner conflict and burden only when we have looked renunciation directly in the face and persuaded ourselves that it is essential for the fulfillment of

Love Thyself Properly

our true and permanent happiness. The scientist renounces worldly fame for the unrewarding quest of truth; the stoic martyr bears the tortures of Fascist bullies rather than betray his cause; the idealist braves the wrath of the mob in the service of uncompromising morality; the people of Israel turns its back upon spiritual appeasement and physical security in order to remain true to the one God of the universe and His moral laws; all these are examples of creative renunciation. Persons who have made such renunciation have learned to live not for the fleeting and perishable ecstasy of the moment, but for the eternal and abiding values which alone are the sources of self-respect and peace of mind.

Acceptance of Self

Another road to proper self-regard is the road of acceptance —the acceptance of our imperfections as well as our perfections. Most men have a dual interpretation of themselves— two pictures of their two selves in separate rooms. In one room are hung all of the portraits of their virtues, done in bright, splashing, glorious colors, but with no shadows and no balance. In the other room hangs the canvas of self-condemnation—a kind of grotesque Dorian Gray caricature—painted equally as unrealistically with dark and morbid greens, blacks, and no lights or relief.

Instead of keeping these two pictures isolated from one another, we must look at them together and gradually blend them into one. In our exalted moods we are afraid to admit guilt, hatred, and shame as elements of our personality; and in our depressed moods we are afraid to credit ourselves with the goodness and the achievement which really are ours.

We must begin now to draw a new portrait and accept and know ourselves for what we are. We are relative, and not *absolute,* creatures; everything we do is tinged with imperfection. So often people foolishly try to become rivals of God and make demands of themselves which only God could make of Himself—rigid demands of absolute perfection. There *is* a little tyrant and a touch of the critic and martyr in all of us. There *are* moments when we want to dominate, to tear down, and to make others suffer. These traits, however, can be and must be subordinated to the total goodness of the personality.

Many people are miserable because they think that occasional destructive feelings necessarily make them terrible persons. But just as Aristotle maintained, "One swallow does not make spring," we must understand that one or two or even a dozen unadmirable traits do not necessarily make an unadmirable person. Long ago Edmund Burke warned humanity about the danger of false generalization in society; of judging a whole race by a few undesirable members. Today we should likewise become aware of the danger of generalization about our individual personality. A splendid freedom awaits us when we realize that we need not feel like moral lepers or emotional pariahs because we have some aggressive, hostile thoughts and feelings toward ourselves and others. When we acknowledge these feelings we no longer have to pretend to be that which we are not. It is enough to be what we *are!* We discover that rigid pride is actually the supreme foe of inner victory, while flexible humility, the kind of humility that appears when we do not demand the impossible or the angelic of ourselves, is the great ally of psychic peace.

Love Thyself Properly

How easily we accept the fact that this is a varied world, with many races, cultures, mores. In America we rejoice in this diversity, this pluralism, which makes up the rich pattern of our national being. We should learn to accept this pluralism in ourselves, to rejoice in the truth that we human beings consist of a variety of moods, impulses, traits, and emotions. Such an attitude would give a deeper significance to Stevenson's childlike thought that "The world is so full of a number of things, I'm sure we should all be as happy as kings."

Progress along this line is slow, partial, often discouraging. A New York psychiatrist tells the story of a man whom he had treated for two years for alcoholism. One day the patient appeared at the analytic session with the news that, on the day before, he had been fired from his job. "You know, doctor," he said, "a year ago if this had happened I wouldn't have been able to take it. I'd have got good and drunk. In fact, I wanted to last night. But somehow I realized that if I could accept this failure without terror, look at it for what it was, I'd be a lot better off in general. I mean that failure, just like success, is one of the great experiences; it's human."

The doctor took this as a sign of distinct advance in the patient's attitude toward life. In a different line of endeavor this patient later went ahead with astounding success, proving that the doctor's prognosis was correct. If a man has learned to love life with all of its facets, neither failure nor success can permanently hurt him.

If we become pluralistic in thinking about ourselves, we shall learn to take the depressed mood or the cruel mood or the unco-operative mood for what it is, one of many, fleeting, not permanent. As pluralists we take ourselves for worse as well as for better, cease demanding a brittle perfection which can lead only to inner despair. There are facets of failure in every person's make-up and there are elements of success. Both must be accepted while we try to emphasize the latter through self-knowledge.

The attainment of proper self-love must become the concern of every wise religion because as long as human beings are enslaved to wrong attitudes toward themselves they cannot help expressing wrong attitudes toward others. If the self is not loved, how can the neighbor be loved as oneself?

That Unique and Loving Potential, You

It occurs to me that we have perhaps been intimidated by the idealized portrait of human nature that much of Western religion has presented to us. And since one of man's profoundest needs is the need for conformity, we have lied to ourselves about our own natures in order to conform to that artificial, unrealistic ideal. This conflict is one of the greatest causes of our discontent, and we must solve it before we can hope to attain peace of mind.

We must begin by firmly believing that "self" is the unique and loving potential in each man that society tries too often to crush. And we must resist with all the powers at our command the oppressive and destructive bands of conformity that cripple us psychically as surely as the feet of a Chinese woman used to be crippled from birth.

I believe that man is infinitely potential, and that given the proper guidance there is hardly a task he cannot perform or a degree of mastery in work and love that he cannot attain.

Love Thyself Properly

However, it must be realized that between our potential and actual attainments there is a whole world of culture that the individual must assimilate. It is during this process of assimilation, this "acculturation period," that things go awry. Actually, our educational system (and this includes the home, the school, the church, and all other cultural forces) tends to submerge the individuality, the selfness, the true potential, of each man. The unique strength of the individual, his bents and leanings, are hardly ever understood or taken into consideration. Mother scolds him for asking too many "whys"; father spanks him for staying out too late "exploring" a local granite quarry; teacher makes him stay after school for drawing a picture of a boat he's interested in, rather than learning his multiplication tables. By infinitely multiplying this necessity to conform, at the expense of developing the individual, unique "self," society succeeds in making a man "good." By frustrating his potential in numberless ways from the time he is born till the time he dies, civilization instills in him a pattern which is so rigid that he is often unable to express his true self at all.

Not that this unwillingness to let him develop is conscious on the part of a man's teachers. They think they are doing a good job. But it is only the individual who holds on to the idea of his true selfhood, who achieves victory at last. And the price he has to pay for his struggle is usually tremendously high. The Shelley who would not be "educated out of" his poetic birthright in the English public-school system; the young stutterer who walked from Chicago to New York to become psychoanalyzed and root out his defect—both paid high prices in personal misery, but they held on to their ideas of who they were and what they *could* be, under circumstances which would have vanquished lesser fighters for the self.

It will help us to make peace with ourselves if we realize that in this battle for self-discovery we need not emerge either a genius or a saint. It will be enough if we hang two comforting mottoes on the inner walls of our individual souls. First is "Respect thyself." The second, "Trust thyself." Respect yourself with all your shortcomings and achievements. Trust yourself to master the undesirable traits of your character and to achieve both relative inner decency and outer confidence. Such knowledge and trust will tend to eliminate our all-too-human tendency to self-contempt. They will be fertile sources of that true love of self which neither exaggerates its powers nor minimizes its worth.

CHAPTER FOUR

Love or Perish!

THE divine commandment "Thou shalt love thy neighbor as thyself" has an engaging sweetness about it—a human tenderness quite at variance with some of the more austere precepts of the Hebrew Bible. Religion has eagerly seized upon this notion of neighborly love, burnished it with affectionate hands throughout the ages, striving to keep it bright in the midst of discouraging darkness and enveloping fear. It may sound absurd to speak of love in a world mad with strife—but the struggle has not been unavailing. If at critical times man's inhumanity to man seemed to gain ascendency, there has always been a Hillel, a Francis of Assisi, a Pasteur, or a Nightingale to remind us that the chief intimation of our immortality is our unique human power for loving our fellow man.

True, modern individualistic morality has overtly and covertly challenged this heaven-sprung concept of neighborly love. In politics and economics—those typical activities of man the earth-treader—we have been deeply indoctrinated with the notion that the individual is a neatly sealed unit, impervious to outer influences. Man, according to this theory, is a kind of self-feeding spring, the generator of his own energies. The philosophy underlying modern capitalism is the economic variant of "Each man for himself, and the devil take the hindmost." In the struggle for survival (a concept borrowed from the purely animal world) we are taught that each man must rely solely on his own strength—live by dint of his own ruthlessness. And as a comforting corollary we are told that if each individual thinks only of himself and his own welfare, the welfare of the society will (incidentally) be advanced.

Quite apart from its ethical callousness, this idea is a fallacy —outmoded, discredited, untrue. Rugged individualism has received many a blow in recent decades from the hammers of economics and politics. Philosophy also has been busily pointing out the errors of "competitive egoism," as Dean Woodbridge calls it. The best modern thinking contends that man can no more exist by and for himself alone than he can live without breathing.

The first fundamental truth about our individual lives is the indispensability of love to every human being. By "love" I mean relatedness to some treasured person or group, the feeling of belongingness to a larger whole and of being of value to other men. The source of all the basic anxieties in human nature is a feeling of being alone and helpless in a hostile world, and the first compulsion of life is the weaving of a stable pattern of relationship between ourselves and our parents and all of those who in time take the place of our parents—the beloved, the friend, the co-worker. Science, as a matter of fact, teaches us today that we can understand the universe only in terms of relatedness, that things are nothing in themselves, in isolation, that even the atom has significance only in some pattern of organization. Carbon atoms. for ex-

Love or Perish!

ample, form charcoal when related in one way and become diamonds when related in another. Everywhere we turn in the laboratory, whether in physics or chemistry or biology or in psychology, we find that isolation is what is impossible and that relationship is everything. A lone atom is a meaningless atom. A related atom is the building stone of nature. A lone human being is a destroyer of values; a related human being is the builder of individual and social peace.

The real progress in the world is not "the self-creating society" but rather "the society creating the self." Thinkers like John Dewey and George Herbert Mead have exploded the eighteenth-century idea that the individual is endowed at birth with a "mind" by means of which he enters into social relations. These philosophers maintain that the individual *achieves* a mind through the social influence of language and the group impact on the plastic growing substance of our personality.

Thus, our interdependence with others is not a matter of religious idealism at all. It is the most encompassing fact of human reality. "Thou shalt have relations with thy neighbors" is a law of psychological life, and many of our most difficult problems arise from the operation of this law. If we understand this relatedness, we shall get on noticeably better with our family, friends, business associates—and ourselves. The revolutionary clinical work of Freud and his successors emphasizes a new truth in that we are literally *made* by our contacts with others! Not merely our minds, but our personalities, emotions, and the whole hierarchy of our values are the result of the influences of focal personalities upon our being. Because we are late arrivals upon the scene of meaning, we are dependent upon others not only for our food and shelter, but also for our cultural and intellectual attainment, our character, our very "selves."

We gradually become what we are by a process of identification with others. Specifically, we are—to an unsuspected extent—what our fathers and mothers, sisters and brothers, uncles and aunts and cousins were before us. Modern psychology demonstrates that with the very milk we drink, we not only ingest physical nutriment, but also swallow the patterns, ideals, reactions, and attitudes of those around us. In a spiritual sense, we digest our heroes and heroines and make their way of life part of our own emotional substance. For man, of all the creatures on earth, has the greatest power of imitation and identification with others. This power is responsible both for the tragedy and for the glory of our existence.

Believe and remember this: every saint and every sinner affects those whom he will never see, because his words and his deeds stamp themselves upon the soft clay of human nature everywhere. A boy catches the contagion of courage from his father, or receives the misery of fear from his mother. Literature abounds with illustrative material. Young Telemachus, Ulysses' son, inherited from his warrior father a bravery that kept Ithaca intact during his father's wanderings. Gogol describes the almost godlike devotion inspired in Taras Bulba's sons by the old father's passionate example of love and hardihood. Ibsen's *Ghosts* is a study of a weak son too greatly influenced by his fear-ridden mother. Countless instances of identification, good and bad, are found in every dramatist from Euripides to O'Neill. Modern psychology has verified the intuitions possessed by world-famous writers, and

Love or Perish!

has shown that we all take other persons inside ourselves to make them part of our soul fabric.

This discovery of the subtle and often unconscious process of identification means that we are never alone and never isolated; that much more than we would like to believe, we are the creations of our environment and the products of our heroes and heroines. Our personality, far from being a self-created substance, is a fabric woven on the loom of other personalities from the cradle to the grave. The mansion of our soul is built out of bricks that others have provided for our use. Incidentally, psychoanalysis proves beyond a shadow of a doubt that modern philosophers, from Berkeley to Bertrand Russell, have needlessly tortured themselves with the idea that man is an isolated organism, excluded from real communication with his fellows. Indeed, Freud, in blasting this idea of human aloneness, has revivified the intuitive wisdom of the prophets of Israel who sang the song of man's relatedness to man.

Since we are formed psychologically by our parents and teachers, so inevitably we mold others. It is not merely what we do, but what we *are* that influences our whole environment. Our isolated acts of charity or cruelty mean little; it is our whole personality structure that is all-important. Our moods, our gestures, the tone of our voice, mold the emotional attitudes of children and adults within the orbit of our influence. Other people become what they are by identification and imitation of us. There is, therefore, a new ethical duty which falls upon all of us—to become free, loving, warm, co-operative, affirmative personalities.

Despite the precept that man cannot pull himself up by his

boot straps, psychology shows us that we can make consistent and gratifying gains in the direction of love, warmth, and tolerance. And the first step in making these valuable gains is to understand the nature of the barriers that keep us from a free and happy intercourse with our neighbors, families, and friends.

The first of these barriers is hate masquerading as love.

Hatred Masked as Love

There is a fearful struggle going forward in the world today —the struggle between love and hatred. This conflict colors the lives of nations and individuals; it is deep, critical, and may well be fatal. Sigmund Freud, the shrewdest analyst of our civilization and its disorders, has commented upon the grim battle between the forces of love (Eros) and the forces of aggressive self-destruction (hate). He says: "The fateful question of the human species seems to be whether . . . it will succeed in mastering derangement of life caused by the human instincts of aggression and self-destruction. Men have brought their powers of subduing nature to such a pitch that by using them they could easily exterminate one another to the last man. They know this—hence arises a great part of their current unrest, their dejection, their mood of apprehension. *And now it may be expected that the other of the two heavenly forces, eternal Eros, will put forth his strength so as to maintain himself alongside of his equally immortal adversary"* (hate).

As we look at the world today, we certainly can find much to justify the cynical conclusion that it is natural to hate

Love or Perish!

rather than to love. How consuming the hatred in war, and the inhumanity of men to their brothers! Under the hypnotic spell of mass violence and exterminatory bombing, it is understandable that we should grow discouraged about man's capacity to love his brothers. We not only see obvious hatred striding across the world, but we also confront countless instances of concealed hatred in the relations between men—hatred which is the more difficult to detect because it hides itself under the mantle of love.

It has always been so! Torquemada, at the time of the Inquisition, no doubt persuaded himself that he was burning heretics at the stake because he loved their immortal souls. This same "inquisitorial love" has reflected itself in much of human history. Wherever you find self-righteous men and women imposing their view coercively upon others (always, of course, under the guise of "doing good"), there you have human aggression and frustration wearing the mantle of love. Fathers and mothers are often inquisitors in this sense, when they force their children into the submissive role of acquiescing in parental authority to the exclusion of discussion and independent thought. Or whenever they impose their fears and prejudices upon their children in the name of education and training—there, too, is vanity masquerading as love.

One of the best illustrations in literature of this counterfeit love is found in Samuel Butler's *The Way of All Flesh.* Theobald, the father, and Christina, the mother, did not want a child and in their hearts they rejected their little son, Ernest. How superbly Butler illustrates the subtle frustrations which these parents inflict upon the child and the equally subtle cruelties which they perpetrate under the guise of stern love.

Peace of Mind

The parents never admitted to themselves how bitterly they resented this new responsibility and how effectively they were venting their anger upon the child, all in the name of duty. To quote Butler: "Christina's version of the matter was that there had never yet been two parents so self-denying and devoted to the highest welfare of their children as Theobald and herself."

Many parents do not realize that they are treating their children as they were treated by their parents, thus achieving a long-deferred revenge for the indignities they endured. They claim that they are stern and rigid with their children out of love, but such love is often a mask behind which lurks deep hostility, rejection, or frustration. Curious confirmation of this comes from the realm of anthropology. Abram Kardiner, in *The Psychological Frontiers of Society,* points out that the Alorese, primitive inhabitants of the Dutch East Indies, systematically deprive their children of any love or care. He shows that the parents unconsciously hate their children because they themselves never received any love from their elders. In direct contrast are the Comanche Indians—a primitive but loving society in which the children have wonderfully integrated egos because their parents are lavish with affection and interest.

In the marriage relationship also there are many counterfeit forms of love. Whenever you find a husband coercing his wife into the surrender of her individuality, or being forced to capitulate to the idiosyncrasies and vanities of the mate, there you have a spurious and false form of "love." "Love" is an honorific term, and men and women like to pretend to themselves that they are showing love when as a matter of

Love or Perish!

fact they are displaying possessiveness, jealousy, power, aggression.

Does all this mean that the possibilities of a love relationship between ourselves and others is an illusion? Has religion been preaching a dream gospel when it has commanded man to love his brothers? There have been those who scoffed at this commandment, labeling it Utopian, impossible. Heine, the poet, was only half in jest when he described his notion of happiness. "My wishes," he said, "are a humble dwelling with a thatched roof, a good bed, good food, flowers at my windows, and some fine tall trees before my door. And if the good God wants to make me completely happy he will grant me the joy of seeing six or seven of my enemies hanging from the trees."

There is a gruesome truth behind Heine's wish. Most of us would like to see our enemies defeated and punished, and it is an ironic human truth that many of us unconsciously entertain the same feeling about our friends and the members of our family. For there is a curious ambivalence about the human soul: it can love and hate the same object at the same time with almost equal force. Society suspects this. It half realizes that civilization is perpetually menaced because of this primary hostility of men toward one another. Therefore, culture has to summon every possible reinforcement against these aggressive hatreds. Hence the ideal command to love one's neighbor as oneself. This commandment is the strongest defense against human hatred, and even though it is impossible to fulfill it completely, men cling to it. For they unconsciously realize that if this commandment were to be swept away, the world would be a place of chaos and desolation.

Peace of Mind

On the positive side, we can derive a tremendous hopefulness from summoning up recollections of heroes and martyrs who really loved humanity, and of ordinary men and women (known to all of us) who sacrifice themselves in unsung ways for the common good of mankind. The amazing courage and self-sacrificing devotion to each other of the Jews of the Warsaw ghetto, and the sense of mutual belongingness among the pioneering builders of contemporary Palestine, are vivid evidence of man's capacity to love his neighbor. And the unanimous testimony of men who have fought together on land, sea, or air is that the individual almost disappears in the group merging of common hazards and goals.

Not every woman can be a Joan of Arc or a Madame Curie, but there are millions of women who make their heroic stand in the patient, uncelebrated fortress of the home. Hundreds of millions of men go down daily into the salt mines of fortitude and duty. Anyone who has worked in fields or mill must remark the unspoken but very active love that animates laborers engaged in the common task. They have among them an *entente cordiale,* exclusive, perhaps, and certainly suspicious of outsiders, but operative, nevertheless, for each other in a roughly tender comradeship, envied by all who have observed it.

Give All to Love

All literature records the yearning of man for love. It is the single greatest theme of Western poetry. Our noblest poets at their highest moments have described the joys of fulfilled love and the wretched suffering visited upon those who lose or lack this most desired of attachments. Individual readers

Love or Perish!

have their own favorite passages to which they turn for solace
and reassurance. The lines I particularly cherish are from
Emerson:

Give all to love;
Obey thy heart;
Friends, kindred, days,
Estate, good-fame,
Plans, credit and the Muse,—
Nothing refuse.

Give all to love! Nothing refuse! If men could obey those
simple injunctions, how quickly and completely the world
would be regenerated! But even if these higher reaches of
fulfillment are denied to most of us, there are lower forms of
love that can be practiced between man and man, employer
and employee, friend and friend. I refer to the humble virtue
of simple kindness, dearness of brother to brother, mutual
tenderness. Next to bread, this is the food all mortals most
hunger for; it is the one essential vitamin of the soul. In times
of catastrophe and disaster it finds a natural expression, good
to contemplate in men's actions.

Too few of us pour this anointing oil on the relationships
of our daily lives. We cannot afford to forget that the superb
charter of kindliness includes salespersons, our own domestic
help, the garage mechanic, and the tailor who presses our
clothes. Too many of us deal in high-sounding platitudes
about the "brotherhood of man," but exhibit an ugly class
consciousness by treating the janitor as though he belonged
to an inferior breed. "I call no man charitable," said Thoreau,
"who forgets that his barber, cook and hostler are made of the
same human clay as himself." We are destroying our own

Peace of Mind

peace of mind when we make dictatorial or bad-tempered aggressions upon the dozens of human beings who help turn the complex wheels of our society. The brotherhood of man will work better when we take the time, patience, and *love* to discover what our fellow man looks like, to learn his name, and to regard him as a human being.

Before we can honestly breathe the word "love" we must acquire a deeper understanding of the immortal hope that originally inspired it, and the *mortal* obligations that keep it alive. The jeweled pivot on which our lives must turn is the deep realization that every person we meet in the course of a day is a dignified, essential human soul and that we are being guilty of gross inhumanity when we snub or abuse him.

Too few of us realize that what the law of gravity is to stars and sun the law of love is to men and women, what attraction and repulsion are in space, approval and rejection are in human society.

The primary joy of life is acceptance, approval, the sense of appreciation and companionship of our human comrades. Many men do not understand that the need for fellowship is really as deep as the need for food, and so they go throughout life accepting many substitutes for genuine, warm, simple relatedness. The Don Juans eternally seeking some new object of passion, the men and women desperately trying to lose themselves in drink, promiscuity, sensuality—in all of the excess of flesh and power—are, more often than we suspect, lonely children lost and naked in a world that has never woven a garment of love for them and that has relentlessly driven them down the empty corridors of the years, desolate and alone. Penetrate behind the mask of men of ruthlessness and

Love or Perish!

of power who seem to move from conquest to conquest, and it will often be seen that their soul is really an army in retreat, fleeing from loneliness to loneliness.

As individuals we require first of all the exchange of simple affection with other human beings. This is the secret of friendship and of marriage—which at its best is mutual encouragement and the assuaging of the wounds that life inflicts on all of us. When we are accepted, approved, *needed* by those who know all about us and like us anyway, we have the first inkling of the peace that transcends understanding.

Dynamic psychology indicates today that in the very nature of man there is not only an unconquerable urge to receive love from others, an inability to live with serenity and joy when deprived of affection from our fellows. But what is more important, there is an inner necessity to give love and to bestow affection upon the outer world.

There comes a time in the development of every ego when it *must* love its neighbors or become a twisted and stunted personality. The normal mature man and woman has within him a surplus "urge to give." Men and women desire children out of their marriage, and that very desire in the human heart is the best proof of an overflowing quality of generosity that is inherent in human nature. The parent is driven by the irresistible desire to add something to life, no longer to receive something from life.

Man's restless yearning to give something of himself, whether it be a physical child or a spiritual child—the child of his mind—a bridge, a poem, a song, an invention, a cure for disease—is the true answer to all cynics and pessimists who maintain that man is total selfishness.

Peace of Mind

There comes a time in the development of ourselves when receiving from others, which is the essence of selfishness, gives way to the irresistible urge to give to others—to grow beyond the limits of one's own skin, whether in the creation of a family or the building of a good society. We reach a point when we become satiated with ourselves and when life demands that we turn outward toward other human life. Then we cease being the passive vessel and ourselves become the living spring. Life does not ask us our wishes on this matter, but in the very process of our very biological maturation it forces us to renounce our status as parasites upon life and summons us to become the patrons of life.

The science of psychology not only maintains that the drive to give love to the world is an inevitable facet of mature human nature, but it also insists that man has an innate need for a world of independent human personalities outside the dominion of his own ego.

It is becoming ever clearer that when we live such self-centered lives as to try to force everyone else into loving or admiring us, we find ultimately that we can enjoy neither ourselves nor others. We just cannot have full human relations unless we respect the independent existence of other human beings. The worst that could befall us would be if we were free and all other people were our slaves. No "self" is possible without a world of freedom. A world where a man is an absolute dictator over everybody else would be literally a mad world. Psychological experiment now indicates that the "love of neighbor" is an inescapable prerequisite for "love of self."

One of the most brilliant psychologists of modern times, Paul Schilder, maintains that the destructive and the cruel

Love or Perish!

aspect of human nature is only a subordinate part of the story; that the main impulse of man is constructive and creative. He tells of the experiment carried on with little children. They were given a number of dolls, with many provocative opportunities for tearing the dolls apart. Yet it was found again and again that the children were driven by the desire to put the figures together again; "to restore the original situation." What often appears to be aggressive cruelty on the part of children is really a driving curiosity and the desire to find out the truth about that independent world outside.

The curiosity on the part of the child, the creative instinct on the part of the adult, are not mere drives to power; they are also manifestations of the inherently constructive and loving traits of human nature. The world is so made that man cannot realize himself fully and cannot satisfy the demands of his own spirit until he satisfies the urge to give to others that lies within his nature, until he helps to establish the freedom and the integrity of his fellow men. Sadism certainly does not tell the whole story about man; it merely indicates that men and women destroy and hate out of a feeling of their own hopelessness and frustration, out of a desire to take vengeance upon the world for their own inner distortions and emotional conflicts. Again and again it is being demonstrated in psychological clinics that when these distortions and conflicts are resolved, the basic trend in human nature toward love and the affirmation of other personalities manifests itself.

Tolerance Is Love

How can we best love our neighbors? Many are the pathways that men choose to follow in their pursuit of altruism. I need mention but one or two. We best show our love for our neighbors when we achieve an inner tolerance for the uniqueness of others, when we resist the temptation to private imperialism. As a matter of fact, the world is full of private imperialists, those who cannot conquer any foreign territory but who make those nearest and dearest to them pay tribute all of their lives to their tyrannical decrees—the father, for example, who forces his artistic son into his business, or the mother who rivets her daughter to her service by chains of pity and guilt, subtly refusing the daughter a life of her own. In contrast to these totalitarians within the family circle we show love to those closest to us when we permit them to be themselves rather than to submit to the strait-jacket of our dominating desires—when we refuse in the name of love ever to demand unconditional surrender from our son, our daughter, our wife, our brother.

A love of neighbor manifests itself in the tolerance not only of the opinions of others but, what is more important, of the *essence* and *uniqueness* of others, when we subscribe to that religious philosophy of life which insists that God has made each man and woman an individual sacred personality endowed with a specific temperament, created with differing needs, hunger, dreams. This is a variegated, pluralistic world where no two stars are the same and every snowflake has its own distinctive pattern. God apparently did not want a regimented world of sameness. That is why creation is so manifold. So is it with us human beings. Some are born dynamic and restless; others placid and contemplative. One man's body is that of a wrestler's—thick-muscled, strong, vibrant, needing far greater physical outlet than does the pale poet or the gaunt

Love or Perish!

ascetic. One man's temperament is full-throated with laughter; another's tinkles with the sad chimes of gentle melancholy. Our physiques are different, and that simple difference oft-times drives us into conflicting fulfillment of our natures, to action or to thought, to passion or to denial, to conquest or to submission. There is here no fatalism of endowment. We can change and prune and shape the hedges of our being, but we must rebel against the sharp shears being wielded by other hands, cutting off the living branches of our spirits in order to make our personalities adornments for their dwellings.

The achievement of true tolerance in personal relations is a prerequisite not only in ethics but also in individual adjustment. As long as we are unhappy if others do not conform to our wishes and our ideas of what is proper, good, acceptable, we show that we ourselves are not certain of the rightness of our inner pattern. He who is sure of himself is deeply willing to let others be themselves. He who is unstable in his own character must reassure himself by trying to compress others into his mold.

We display true love for our neighbors when we cease to demand that another person become a modified version of our ideas—a revised edition of ourselves.

Tolerance, which is one form of love of neighbor, must manifest itself not only in our intimate personal relations, but also in the arena of society as well. In the world of opinion and politics, tolerance is that virtue by which liberated minds conquer the evils of bigotry and hatred. Tolerance implies more than forbearance or the passive enduring of ideas differing from our own. Properly conceived, *tolerance is the positive and cordial effort to understand another's beliefs, practices, and habits without necessarily sharing or accepting them.* Tolerance quickens our appreciation and increases our respect for a neighbor's point of view. It goes even further; it assumes a militant aspect when the rights of an opponent are assailed. Voltaire's dictum, "I do not agree with a word that you say, but I will defend to the death your right to say it," is for all ages and places the perfect utterance of the tolerant ideal.

A delicate balance must be struck by the tolerant man, a balance between unreasoned hatred—grounded in ignorance and fear—and pale indifferentism, which may be merely a symptom of spiritual sloth. "Much that passes for Tolerance," says John Morley, "is only a pretentious form of being without settled opinions of our own, or any desire to settle them." Tolerance is *not* moral laxity or easy deviation from established principles. If we say apathetically, "One notion is as good as another," we are not being tolerant; we are merely being lazy. Yet if we attempt to force our neighbor to conform to our convictions, we run the gravest of all risks—the risk of violating the rights of others.

Inspired guides in these matters—John Milton in England and Roger Williams in our own country—recommend neither a mealy-mouthed acquiescence nor a cocksure pugnacity. Emphatically *not* the latter. Dense, unenlightened people are notoriously confident that they have the monopoly on truth; if you need proof, feel the weight of their knuckles. But anyone with the faintest glimmerings of imagination knows that truth is broader than any individual conception of it, stronger than any fist. Recall, too, how many earnestly held opinions and emotions we have outgrown with the passage of years. Given a little luck, plus a lively sense of the world about us,

Love or Perish!

we shall probably outgrow many more. Renan's remark that *our opinions become fixed at the point where we stop thinking* should be sufficient warning against premature hardening of our intellectual arteries, or too stubborn insistence that we are infallibly and invariably right.

Viewed in this way, tolerance becomes the bulwark of social and individual liberty, the guarantor of a hundred civil rights, and the chief element in any cultural advance that a society may expect to make. Undermine tolerance or whittle it away, and you diminish the traditional liberties we so arduously struggled for and endanger the fight for the freedoms still to be won. Our free press, our privileges of free assembly and religious worship, our very form of democratic government, are supported by dikes of tolerance, laboriously built, privately held, and individually practiced. When we relax our private grasp of tolerance, when we fail to practice it in our individual lives, we jeopardize the structure for all.

There have been some great apostles of tolerance in America; George Washington's intervention in behalf of the Tories is a little-known example. When patriotic hotheads wished to plunder Tory estates and do violence to their persons, Washington permitted the Tories to depart peaceably for Canada. Demanding liberty for conscience himself, Washington defended it in others. Roger Williams, denied religious liberty in Salem, made a hazardous trek on foot through wintry forests to found Providence, the first sanctuary of civil and religious tolerance in America. Phillips Brooks, in a famous sermon, condensed his philosophy of American tolerance in these words: "It expresses a perfectly legitimate and honorable relation between opposite minds. I disagree with my friend. But

Peace of Mind

I respect him; I want him to be true to his convictions yet I claim the right and duty of trying to persuade him to my belief. Tolerance is the meeting in perfect harmony of earnest conviction and personal indulgence."

But despite the hardihood of its occasional champions, tolerance itself is a fragile plant. Untended, it withers and dies. As it fades, another growth—the poisonous mushroom of *intolerance*—takes its place. This does not happen suddenly, but by imperceptible degrees. A privilege is shorn away, a censorship erected, a hatred takes root, oppressive legislation is enacted, and soon we are living in the black forest of intolerance, sunless and fearsome for all who dwell in its shade.

Democracy is the principle of tolerance extended into the sphere of politics. Tolerance *preserves*, rather than destroys, minorities. And these minorities in turn perform a valuable function by acting as a brake upon the party in power. This is a major premise of our government. Take away tolerance and our democracy will not survive.

Religion and Love

The task of religion, as far as love and hate are concerned, is immensely clarified by the discoveries of dynamic psychology. Men no longer should be exhorted to altruism but should be taught to recognize the face of self-hate in all its guises of both narcissism and masochism. Religion now can teach man the inner origins of warped attitudes toward the self; it can teach him how to overcome these distorting enemies of inner peace. Religion can remove the mask from false love of others

Love or Perish!

which actually is sadism in disguise. It can teach us to become sensitive and subtle in our understanding of the meaning of love, counterfeit and real. And it can strengthen us in the conviction that love of neighbor is no illusion but is part of the ultimate compulsion of the human universe.

Religion can now help us understand that people who want always to receive and never to give are cases of arrested development. They are to be pitied and helped to develop, just as we take stunted children with glandular defects and through hormone injections and endocrine extracts enable them to mature physically. The time must come when we shall be subtle enough to see with the eye of our imagination the soul of the selfish man as we now can see the stunted physique of the abnormal man. Then we shall realize that the totally self-centered individual is really a moral cretin, a spiritual imbecile—that he who tries to take but not to give to life inevitably dies half a man.

Religion illumined by modern psychology can now teach men the meaning of "love," immature and mature. Love is not mature when it presents to the "self" a reparations bill for the indemnity of past defects, a reparations bill that the human ego can no more pay than an impoverished and vanquished nation can satisfy a vengeful victor. When we demand of ourselves extreme perfection, extreme independence, extreme saintliness, extreme power—then, no matter how much attention we may lavish upon our mind and spirit, we are loving ourselves the way the inquisitor loves the heretic that he is burning.

Mature love of our neighbor is unconditional love which does not ask the impossible, but which understands that the ideal of life is tolerant growth, flexible mutuality, and progressive harmony. Love becomes mature when it achieves the attitude of respect for the valuable aspects of the "self" and the "neighbor." A man who is capable of treasuring the constructive and creative aspects of his own personality, who sees them as part of a larger social inheritance, is willing both to give and to receive affection without seeking to make himself the master over others or the slave of others—such a man has entered the holy of holies of genuine adult love.

CHAPTER FIVE

Fear Wears Many Masks

THIS is a dangerous world in which we live, and no normal person can face life without experiencing countless fears and worries. They are part of the fee we pay for citizenship in an unpredictable universe. But if it is normal for us to experience fear and worry, it is also possible to master these enemies of serenity. Man's greatest triumph, Bertrand Russell declares, in *A Free Man's Worship,* is to achieve stability and inner repose in a world of shifting threats and terrifying change.

In a certain sense, man is blessed by his capacity to know fear. We could not survive at all if we did not have a fear mechanism to sound the alert when menacing bombs, disease germs, or social and moral pitfalls threaten our well-being. It is good that we know how to grow afraid, because there *are* fearful objects and hostile forces that we must all learn to avoid or conquer if we are to survive.

All of the inventions and discoveries of human civilization are in a sense by-products of our fears and worries. Men were afraid of the dark. They learned the art of fire and discovered the secrets of electricity. Men were afraid of pain—and that fear became the mother of medicine and all the discoveries of surgery, anesthesia, and healing. If we were to take away man's capacity to fear, we would take away, also, his capacity to grow, since fear is often the stimulus to growth, the goad to invention.

The truth is that man has to pay the price of fear and worry in order to be human. The beast in the field knows animal terror but is immune to the emotions which man alone experiences because of his sense of imagination and gift of reason. The high price tag of our humanity is attached to the sensitive nerve endings which expose us (as the armored clam is never exposed) to the pain, dangers, and glories of conscious life. At times we rebel at our human lot and envy the dull bivalve, yet if the choice were given to us, there are few among us who would choose to cut the sensitive nerve endings, and make ourselves incapable of fear—for such a severing would render us incapable of love, yearning, and loyalty. Our susceptibility to anxiety is the soil of our human growth, our human dream and vision.

Now, it is true that temperaments differ. The thickness of our emotional skins varies. Some phlegmatic people are able to bear a very heavy burden without breaking under the strain; for others, the load of tension must be much lighter if the mind is to retain its balance. At the same time we must remember that often the most fear-ridden personalities are the most creative personalities. Lincoln and Dostoevsky were haunted by recurrent depressions all their lives, yet they achieved infinitely more for the human race than all of the "blithe spirits" who seem to dance along the highway of existence fearlessly and freely.

No generalization, therefore, can cover all human cases. Yet it is correct to maintain that all human beings without exception—or with the exception of the moron and idiot—experience fear and worry. The pattern may be different, the forms and shapes that the fears assume are extremely variegated, but basically all men and women in one degree or another feel guilty, dread pain, suffer loneliness, seek reassurance. It is merely the conspiracy of silence about our deepest inner feelings, our habit of hiding behind the masks of convention, which prevents us from recognizing the universal brotherhood of anxiety which binds the whole human race together.

There is, of course, a difference between desirable and undesirable fear. Desirable fear is the emotion we experience in the presence of real danger, physical or social. Our soldiers and sailors experienced fear when they went into combat; that very emotion intensified the flow of adrenalin, mobilized their physical and mental energy, and enabled them to meet the objective menace with skill and success. A soldier who did not know how to be afraid was a danger to himself and a menace to his comrades. The fact that our soldiers and sailors and aviators fulfilled their missions *in spite of fear* is one more evidence of man's capacity to use his human endowment for courageous ends.

The same thing is true in civilian life. We experience physical pain. Fear of what it means sends us to our doctor—the warning signal proves to be our friend rather than our foe. The whole world today is confronted with the menace of the atomic bomb, and sensitive men and women throughout the globe are profoundly concerned about the revolutionary implications of this awe-inspiring human discovery. The fear that atomic energy will become a weapon of universal destruction rather than a tool of planetary health and prosperity is a realistic fear—indispensable, as a matter of fact, for the planning of new strategies to master the social and economic dangers of our day. Some fears and worries, then, are necessary, desirable, creative of new individual and collective welfare. These we should not seek to eliminate, unless we are indifferent to survival and progress.

It is the *excessive* fears and neurotic worries which congeal us, reduce our efficiency, heighten the morbidity which we should all seek to master. Just as our endocrine glands, which regulate our physical health, require just the proper amount of secretion, so likewise in our mental life a certain degree of anxiety is normal and healthy. But excessive and neurotic secretions of fear poison and distort our whole nature.

What Is Neurotic Fear?

The best illustration of the difference between normal and neurotic fear was given by Sigmund Freud himself. A person in an African jungle, he said, may quite properly be afraid of snakes. That is normal and self-protective. But if a friend of ours suddenly begins to fear that snakes are under the carpet of his city apartment, then we know that his fear is neurotic, abnormal. In attempting to estimate our own fears we may profitably apply Freud's serviceable yardstick. It would be quite normal for a Polish mother to fear that her children might die of starvation, but when a wealthy American mother comes into my study and tells me that her children are dying of slow malnutrition, I suspect that her fear is a morbid and neurotic shadow, based on her own feelings of guilt, fear, and hatred.

Fear Wears Many Masks

Are not most of our fears so based? Suppose we scrutinize that large body of fears coming under the heading of "personal anxiety." Oftener than not, they turn out to be snakes under the carpet. Sometimes we are afraid about our health and succumb to hypochondriacal moods. We worry about our hearts, our lungs, our blood pressure, our insomnia. We begin to feel our pulse and to find evidence of disease in every innocent or meaningless symptom. If we are not worried about our physical well-being, we are concerned about our personalities. We lack self-confidence, feel insecure, are driven by a sense of inferiority, bemoan our failures, and imagine that we are the object of scorn or disapproval on the part of those whose opinions we value most. We begin to live through the dark night of the soul; the sun of worship and friendship, of love and family, is eclipsed by the shadows of our inner depression.

Our worries about ourselves, our own failures and insecurities, are often carried over into a fancied concern about those who are nearest and dearest to us—our boy overseas, our husband, brother, sister, or daughter—who are in some respects extensions of our own personality. Many a mother who claims to be worrying about her "daughter's morality" is in truth afflicted by unconscious doubts of her own virtue. Every day we hear businessmen attacking the Administration, grumbling about taxes, or worrying about our relations with Russia. These men attribute their gloom and depression to some external remote cause, when the true root of their anxiety lies deep within themselves.

We must realize, of course, that our fears may assume different disguises and wear different uniforms. Sometimes they are dressed in the outfit of mental phobias and attitudes—the

Peace of Mind

fear of high places, of closed rooms. Modern psychology throws many a helpful beam of light into the dark recesses of childhood where our fears originate and makes clear why so many people live lives of apprehension, sometimes hysterically frightened of being alone with themselves, at other times rigidly aloof, afraid of involvement with other human beings, at moments driven to inner trembling at the thought of losing the love of another person or the respect of associates, afraid of being disparaged, rejected, unmasked.

Fear of love turns some women into frigid marble statues; fear of success (yes, many of us are actually afraid to succeed) drives men down the grim roads of drink or the frittering path of Don-Juanism. Karl Menninger, in his brilliant book *Man Against Himself,* asserts that modern man enters into the very complicated conspiracy of fear in order to prevent his successful emergence into maturity and achievement. He loads his soul with fears, saddles himself with guilty worries, simply in order that he may fail!

Cunningly, our fears sometimes cloak themselves in the garments of physical pain. The brilliant new science of psychosomatic medicine has demonstrated that a whole gamut of illnesses, from the common cold to crippling arthritis, can often be traced to deep-seated fears. Of course, artists and novelists knew this long ago. Thomas Mann's epic story *The Magic Mountain* shows how many oversensitive, fearful persons sometimes find refuge in tuberculosis rather than face the battle of actual life. It is so much easier to be sick than courageous! The ill-health enjoyed by many chronic invalids is, we are beginning to learn, nothing more than an elaborate disguise for neurotic fears.

86

Fear Wears Many Masks

Even subtler is a camouflage that fear throws up in the lives of seemingly successful businessmen. Here is a man we all know—financially prosperous, a very captain of trade. Everyone believes in him—that is, everyone but himself. He is never at peace with himself and never believes in the reality of his achievements. He continually tries to build new dikes to ward off the threatening flood of failure. He invests his time, his energy, his skill, ruthlessly driving himself from one financial conquest to another. To all outward appearances, he is a success. As far as his inner feelings are concerned, he is a fear-ridden failure.

Why? Well, somewhere in his childhood he was made to feel little and powerless. In order to prove himself to the adult world, he engaged in some childish venture and failed. The adult world laughed at his efforts. The adults soon forgot their ridicule, but the child never forgot it. He had placed all his trust in that first test of strength and had dreamed of showing his father, his mother, his older brother how competent he was. When he was shown up as a weakling, a failure, his world collapsed at the sound of adult laughter, disapproval, scorn. This was a shock from which the sensitive child really did not recover. In his adult life he was always expecting his commercial ventures, his very career, to collapse. He waited for the ax to fall and never believed in the possibility of his own power. Hence his present insecurity; his inferiority feelings are the story of his childhood fears being repeated again and again on the record of mature strivings.

Here is the woman, brilliantly described by Karen Horney, who suffers from moods of depression. She has a loving husband, two splendid children, a circle of friends, a charming

Peace of Mind

house. Yet she is hopelessly depressed. It is more than absurd to say to her, "All this is imaginary. It's just in your mind." Of course it is just in her mind, but the question is: *why* is it in her mind?

The answer can only be found in tracing back the thread of her character to the time when it first began to be wound on the spool of experience. She was the daughter of a gifted and self-centered mother and a busy, preoccupied physician father. There was a brother three years older than herself. She was unwanted. The mother felt that the coming of this little girl interfered with her social whirl. Nothing was ever said to the child, but she sensed the atmosphere in the home quite well. The mother and her son were extremely close to one another and the little girl desperately tried to break into that charmed circle. Quietly, and quite unconsciously, she was rejected, and in her rejection she felt an enormous rage against life. She tried to express that rage by temper tantrums and was severely punished. She found that she could not get any love unless she concealed her resentment, her anger. Conceal it she did. She bought a rather grudging approval by transforming herself into a docile and perfect little lady. It was then that her mother and her brother gave her the crumbs from the table of their shared devotion. She falsified her nature and made herself into a dependent, hypocritical, subservient creature always carrying a façade concealing her real feelings. She came into adolescence and into maturity living a psychological lie. She had talents of her own. She was afraid to express them because her early attempts at self-assertion had brought pain and rejection. And so, beneath the surface of this woman's life writhed all the serpents of unexpressed rage and resentment which, since her childhood, she had repressed. She had never dared to look at them in the light and it was these serpents of unexpressed rage which succeeded in poisoning her with the fangs of depression.

Here is a portrait of another woman in whom fear cloaked itself in physical disease rather than in mental depression. Left an orphan at the age of four, she was raised by an old grandmother. The grandmother was harsh and forbidding. The child was full of fear but was never permitted to show any anger. She was raised under a very strict moral discipline and found no outlets for her yearning to be loved and appreciated. In order to escape she married quite young—married a wastrel of a husband from whom she also received no real affection. In her early thirties she developed extremely high blood pressure as a result of the continual civil war in her own spirit between her passive, dependent yearning for love, which was never satisfied, and her terrible rage and resentment, which she could not channel or express.

In dealing with the personal fears and worries which come to us in mature life, psychiatry tells us that we should first of all look at them without flinching, and recognize that our childhood is a blackmailer that makes us pay over and over again for some of the failures or mistakes that long ago have been outgrown. We should, in other words, learn that there is a "statute of limitations" not only upon crimes in the courts of society, but also upon the anxieties and the fears of the soul.

Many a feeling of insecurity, of inferiority, is a hangover from that chapter in our life's story when we really *were* inadequate and inferior. There is nothing imaginary about a child's feeling of helplessness—the loss of support as he stumbles

Peace of Mind

across a floor, falls out of an unguarded bed, or seeks in vain to communicate without the tool of language his feelings of pain, of hunger, of loneliness. As children we actually were inadequate and weak. We knew that there was a vast difference between our weakness and the strength of the adult world. But now that we are grown up, such fears are meaningless. As Professor Dollard of Yale so well says, "The world of gigantic efficient parents no longer exists . . . no one is as superior to us as adults as were our parents when we were children." One of the real ways to overcome our fears is to understand and thus remove that "emotional lag" between the actuality of adult accomplishment and our haunting memory of childish weakness.

Colonel Grinker and Major Spiegel, in their new work *Men Under Stress,* point out how important it is to remove this "emotional lag." Aviators suffering from psychic disturbances during and after combat could not be helped by hypnosis or prolonged rest, because neither gave the flier *any new knowledge about himself and his past.* Pilots suffering from neurotic disturbance were cured through the new method of "narco-synthesis" used by the army, whereby the pilots were enabled to delve into their past, to relive in memory not merely the shocks of the war but the earlier conflicts of boyhood and adolescence. When they learned that many a present anxiety was really a residue from some childish need or apprehension, their adult ego was able to digest this new knowledge and to utilize it for renewed courage and psychic health.

All of us cannot, and need not, turn to "narco-synthesis." But we can utilize the insight which shows many of our present anxieties to be merely the disguised and extended shadows of childhood. How comfortingly this knowledge serves us! Suppose we *were* unwanted or rejected by our parents? They do not exhaust the whole world. There are others now in our present experience who want and love and admire us. Shall we, then, reject the present in order to remain incarcerated in the past? Let us look frankly into the mirror of our childhood and see how many of the fears and worries and distortions of our present existence come from that nursery level of life.

Are we obsessed perhaps with a fear of death or the thought of punishment in an afterlife? Let us come to see that such fear is a projection from our early experience when we were punished by our parent, locked in a room, left alone, seemingly deserted. Needlessly, as adults, we read into the whole world that kind of aloneness and punishment which exists only in our childhood phase of development.

Are we afraid of being inferior, continually haunted by the disapproval of others, fearful of social rejection? Let us look at these anxieties in the light of maturity and see that we are just as competent, as good, as attractive, as intelligent as the rest of our very fallible neighbors. Let us realize that we need not measure our value by their yardstick—a yardstick that is just as limited as our own. The world of maturity is a world of mutual interdependence, where others need us just as much as we need them. It is not a world where we should expect to be either loved or punished as we were loved and punished in childhood.

Rage, Aggression, Hostility

Many of our physical and mental disturbances arise from our fear of ourselves!

Peace of Mind

We are afraid of what we will do to others, afraid of the rage that lies in wait somewhere deep in our souls. How many human beings go through the world frozen with rage against life! This deeply hidden inner anger may be the product of hurt pride or of real frustration in office, factory, clinic, or home. Whatever may be the cause of our frozen rage (which is the inevitable mother of depression), the great word of hope today is that this rage can be conquered and drained off into creative channels.

How does this rage originate? Well, as babies we have hungers and needs which at times the mother cannot and at other times ought not to satisfy. Frustrated in the immediate fulfillment of our cries, we grow extremely angry. The hostility born of that frustration reveals itself in temper tantrums which are punished by the adult world. This punishment teaches fear. The dynamics of this fear-generating process is "frustration, anger, punishment for that anger—then fear." We are conditioned to connect anger and fear, as stimulus and response. When in adulthood the life situation realistically demands firmness or aggressiveness on our part, too many ruthlessly suppress the anger behind the mask of fear.

What should we do? We should all learn that a certain amount of aggressive energy is normal and certainly manageable in maturity. Most of us can drain off the excess of our angry feelings and destructive impulses in exercise, in competitive games, or in the vigorous battles against the evils of nature and society. We also must learn that no one will now punish us for the legitimate expression of self-assertiveness and creative pugnacity as our parents once punished us for our undisciplined temper tantrums. Furthermore, let us always remember

Fear Wears Many Masks

that we need not totally repress the angry part of our nature. We can always give it an outlet in the safe realm of fantasy. A classic example of such fantasy is given by Max Beerbohm, who made a practice of concocting imaginary letters to people he hated. Sometimes he went so far as actually to write the letters and in the very process of releasing his anger it evaporated.

As mature men and women we should regard our minds as a true democracy where all kinds of emotions and ideas should be given freedom of speech. If in political life we are willing to grant civil liberties to all sorts of parties and programs, should we not be equally willing to grant civil liberty to our innermost thoughts and drives, confident that the more dangerous of them will be outvoted by the decent and creative majority within our minds? Do I mean that we should hit out at our enemy or our superior whenever the mood strikes us? No, I repeat that I am suggesting quite the reverse—self-control in action based upon self-expression in fantasy.

Sometimes we can talk out our angers with a dear friend, a brother, a religious counselor. At other times we need the expert guidance of the psychiatrist. Strange as it may seem, the person to whom we confide our inner moods may temporarily become the object of our aggression.

This, too, is a profound discovery of modern psychotherapy —that we ofttimes project onto some comrade or counselor in our present existence the feelings of hate, hostility, or fear that we once experienced in relation to a mother, a father, an older brother—feelings that we concealed from ourselves in the early years of our life. We transfer to some contemporaries certain of our moods and reactions, but that very transference, painful though it may prove to be, is an important step in our emotional liberation. After a while we learn to our great relief that we are not really angry at our wife, husband, friend, or physician; they are merely convenient pegs upon which we hang the hostility that we had failed to work out in some previous stage of our development. By his calm patience, the friend or counselor proves to be the physician-artist releasing our pent-up emotions, the temporary victim who becomes the permanent healer.

A source of hope lies also in the fact that our moods are temporary. This is a hard lesson for many people to learn. When we are tired, every pinprick becomes the stab of a knife and every molehill becomes a mountain. It is natural and normal for all of us to have depressed moods. When we enter the tunnel of darkness we forget that there is an exit as well as an entrance, and that we can come out into the light again. We human beings are very tough organisms, able to withstand many shocks, to shed many tears, to live through many tragedies without breaking. Let us learn, then, not to take the depression of the day or the month as the permanent state of our life. It is a brief tunnel of darkness carved into the mountain of light.

In the presence of our personal fears and worries we should all be willing to be helped. There are many people who resist aid, who are ashamed to confess their weakness to anyone else. There are some who perversely hug their fears and phobias to themselves. This is understandable because our fears are sometimes like old friends; we are afraid to give them up because they have a certain psychological premium value. They shield us against reality and the facing of reality. The woman

Fear Wears Many Masks

who goes throughout her life as a semi-invalid unconsciously hates to give up this protecting neurosis. She learned as a child to gain attention and love through illness, and she has used her illness to attract the attention and to rivet the chains of devotion of husband, children, family, and friends. Our fears are often like the illness shield of that woman. They protect us against reality and the necessity of growing up. At the same time, most human beings become dissatisfied with emotional infantilism. There is a drive to grow up in most normal people, a yearning to become adult. That yearning is the basis of our hope for a better and freer humanity.

Yes, we must be willing to be helped, and accept the resources that are now available for such help. These resources are by no means as varied and as accessible as they should be in a wisely ordered society. In fact, one of the great tasks of government and education in the next few years will be to encourage and subsidize great numbers of qualified psychiatrists and psychological clinics throughout America, in small towns as well as in large cities. Yet, even today there are many agencies giving valuable psychological guidance. Veterans' clinics, capable of achieving much in the release of postbattle tensions and the postwar fears of our fighting men, are being established throughout the country. Social workers trained in psychology are on the staff of every welfare agency throughout the country. Many great factories and industrial plants have psychological counselors devoting their whole time to therapy among the workers. The latest housing programs in Oregon, California, and elsewhere include psychological assistance in the fee that the tenant pays for rent. And lastly, enlightened clergymen of every sect and faith are preparing themselves in the fields of psychiatry and mental hygiene, the better to help those among their parishioners who stand in need of wise assistance and guidance. As a matter of record, it is the church and synagogue which—in this most impersonal and technological of eras—are providing the meeting grounds where, in the warmth of fellowship, men and women can find mutual aid and group therapy.

If we want to master fear and worry we must not only be willing to accept help from others but also learn to accept ourselves and our abilities as well as our limitations. In discussing proper self-love I have already pointed out how important it is for us to accept our inadequacies in the realm of emotion, to make peace with our inevitable imperfections so far as our feelings and moods are concerned. At this point I stress the necessity of accepting our imperfections so far as abilities and achievements are concerned. The acceptance of such limitations is enormously difficult for many people. Why is this so? Partly because as children we daydreamed about a thousand different kingdoms that we would conquer; the stories, fables, and fairy tales of childhood emphasized power rather than limitation. In the second place, as children we invested our heroes with omnipotence, possibly as an escape from our own weakness. Lastly, we were tormented by the perfectionism which our parents demanded of us as a result of their inability to accept their own limitations. Many times a mother will project onto her daughter the ambitions that she failed to achieve, demanding that her offspring redeem her failure. Children are often the tragically lengthened shadows of their parents' failures! The parents expect a second chance out of life through the achievement of perfection in their progeny.

Fear Wears Many Masks

We carry, then, the burden of our childhood expectations into maturity. No wonder that we grow afraid, become anxious, feel inferior. No wonder that we develop ulcers, hypertension, and heart conditions out of our restless and haunted compulsion to achieve the absolute. Yet, we will obtain inner peace only when we have declared a truce and made an armistice with the army of our childhood expectations. No one of us escapes limitations. We sometimes are angry, petty, lazy, callous, but we also are kindly, generous, creative. Some people are gifted with their hands, some people are gifted in the realm of art or music, some people are gifted in the realm of abstract ideas. Almost no one is gifted in all three realms. We are all limited, and we must accept ourselves with our limitations, recognizing that we can do what others cannot do, that we can contribute where others cannot contribute.

To accept ourselves with our limitations means also that we will recognize how variable and flexible our lives can be. The great thing about life is that as long as we live we have the privilege of growing. We can learn new skills, engage in new kinds of work, devote ourselves to new causes, make new friends, if only we will exercise a little initiative and refuse to become fixed, rigid, and psychologically arteriosclerotic before our time. Let us, then, learn how to accept ourselves—accept the truth that we are capable in some directions and limited in others, that genius is rare, that mediocrity is the portion of almost all of us, but that all of us can contribute from the storehouse of our skills to the enrichment of our common life. Let us accept our emotional frailties, knowing that every person has some phobia lurking within his mind and that the normal person is he who is willing to accept life with its limitations and its opportunities joyfully and courageously.

Not only must we accept ourselves, but we must also *change ourselves*. Until the day of our death we can change, we can tap hidden resources in our make-up. We can discipline ourselves to turn from the morbid circle of useless self-pity or enslavement to childish frustrations and begin to give of our energy to other people, to a cause, a movement, a great social enterprise. In such service we can find freedom from ourselves and liberty from our fears.

Economic Fears—Real and Unreal

It is natural to experience fear in the outer world concerning our economic and social future. These are not snakes under the carpet, but very real. Many men torment themselves because their businesses have failed, or are failing, or threaten to fail in this reconversion period. Countless people are afraid of unemployment or the collapse of their careers or professions. These are very real anxieties and cannot be dismissed by the magic of words. One of the most terrible things about unemployment is the destruction of pride, the crushing of a man's spirit, the revelation of himself as a failure in the eyes of those whom he wishes to impress most—his wife and his children. In a lesser degree this is the haunting and the gnawing fear among many men in this highly competitive society. They fear that they are not making the grade, that their friends or neighbors are more successful or more powerful than they.

What can be said about these fears and worries? In the first place, multitudes of men and women must realize that the temporary dislocations of industry and commerce do not mean that they personally are failures. Franklin Delano Roosevelt said that our economic machine is so colossal today that men should not blame themselves when factors completely beyond their control temporarily defeat their efforts. No man need feel himself a failure in his own eyes or the eyes of his family if he suffers temporary dislocation, unemployment, or bankruptcy.

But firmly attached to genuine economic fears are highly neurotic residues. Americans particularly are participating in a marathon race in which the runners are extremely anxious about those who are panting at their heels and envious of those whose flying feet outpace them. Dr. Kardiner, in his extremely provocative work, *The Psychological Frontiers of Society,* devotes many pages to an analysis of the drive for success which is the source of many of the breakdowns and premature cardiac deaths in this relentless race for power. Ours is a money culture, there is no doubt about it—and there are large numbers of people in this culture who make acquisition rather than enjoyment their goal in life. They literally kill themselves in the greedy pursuit of more and more wealth. The idolatry of material success has infected all classes in our American society, and the inevitable failure of the vast majority of people to attain luxury and great wealth is responsible for the gnawing sense of insecurity and self-disdain.

The drive to mastery, the yearning for achievement, are admirable attributes of our aspiring human nature. Where, then, do we go wrong? *We err in the excessive energy that we devote not to real accomplishment but to neurotic combat.* To speak cynically, we are still like the Children of Israel dancing around the golden calf. Judaism always understood the danger of this worship of the golden calf. Psychology today can aid religion in giving many people insights into the reason for this neurotic idolatry. The amazing thing is that it is not gold per se which is idolized. The gold is merely the instrument of vengeance, the trusty sword with which to pay off old scores, the dreamed-of armor of invulnerability with which vulnerable children clothe their daydreams. The truth of the matter is that many people are haunted by continual dissatisfaction because their goals are *borrowed goals*. They have taken over their life ambition not only from the culture in which they live, but from some dominant member in the family whose superiority they once resented. Without knowing it, many men and women spend their all-too-short lives slaving away with the unconscious thought, "I am going to be rich enough and powerful enough to get even, to show them all up." Multitudes are really competing with ghosts, with early fraternal or parental rivals. They are never happy because they can never achieve what they want: namely, absolute victory.

There is another neurotic aspect to our money culture—the competitiveness which tears asunder almost every community in America today. A man may have a home, possessions, a charming family, and yet find all these things ashy to his taste because he has been outstripped in the marathon race by some other runners to the golden tape line. It is not that he does not possess enough for his wants but that others possess more. It is the *more* that haunts him, makes him deprecate himself, and minimize his real achievements. This is the cancer eating away at his serenity.

The time has come when a man must say to himself: "I am no longer going to be interested in how much power or wealth

Fear Wears Many Masks

another man possesses so long as I can attain enough for the dignity and security of my family and myself. I am going to break through this vicious circle which always asks the question of life in a comparative degree: 'Who is bigger?' 'Who is richer?' 'Who has more?' I am going to set my goals for myself rather than borrow them from others. I will strive to achieve a mature attitude toward success which is ambition for growth and accomplishment, real accomplishment rather than spurious, decorative, and vanity-filled acquisition. I refuse any longer to destroy my peace of mind by striving after wind, and I will judge myself in the scale of goodness and culture as well as in the balance of silver and gold."

Such a man is on the road to avoiding the neurotic materialism of our age. He is like the poet who does not tear himself to pieces because his sonnet is not equal to that of Shakespeare. He is like the musician who does not always despise his little fugue because it lacks the magic of Bach. He is like the poet or musician who learns to accept himself and to be happy with his own growth from year to year rather than paralyze his gifted pen or his talented ear by contrast with the giants and the immortals.

Psychology will help religion to diminish the worship of the golden calf among men as it aids men to become free of their overexcessive demands upon themselves. When, instead of the pathological race for more houses and jewels, cars and refrigerators, bonds and stocks—so often mere weapons of aggression and vengeance—when, instead of seeking these fictitious goals, men learn a certain modesty about things and become genuinely contented with their real contributions and achievements—only then is serenity achieved. Only when we harness our own creative energies to *goals which are of our own adult choice,* not imposed upon us by the compulsions of unresolved childhood competition, can we call ourselves mature and happy.

This much must be said about our economic anxieties. We must anticipate a certain amount of hardship in these immediate postwar years, but every man and woman should feel that his skill and talent will be needed in the rebuilding of the devastated world. No brain and no muscle will be superfluous in the society of abundance that we are about to create. I believe that the time is coming when mankind will insist not only upon health insurance, old-age insurance, and unemployment insurance, but when the age-old fears of want and poverty, illness and uselessness, will be conquered by the collective conscience of democratic society. Work and status must be guaranteed to every child on earth because we know now that lack of status and of security and the presence of joblessness and hunger can become the percussion cap on the atomic bombs of earth's destruction. We human beings who can invent and produce such incredible machines of war can become and must become no less ingenious in social engineering to eliminate the economic fears in the hearts of men and women.

Metaphysical Fears

Finally, let us turn to the religious and metaphysical fears of men. Throughout the ages sensitive human beings have been afraid of death and oblivion. I do not deny that there are moments when we feel our aloneness and are frightened by our fragility. It is good for us to deepen our natures by reflect-

Fear Wears Many Masks

ing upon the brevity of our life and the vanity of our days. Yet, profound religions like Judaism and Christianity can teach us what we need to know—that we are rooted in the Divine and that we need not fear our destiny either here or in any world yet to come. God has given us powers sufficient for the building of a decent life here on this earth, and if in His wisdom He desires us to live in worlds yet undreamed of, He will give us powers to meet the demands and answer the challenge of that afterlife. We live today with the everlasting arms beneath us: we breathe, we eat, we walk, we think and dream, all because we are sustained by a universe greater than ourselves and preserved by a love beyond our fathoming.

In the book *Burma Diary* the author describes how administering to the bomb-stricken people he finds himself saying to them, " 'God keep you.'...What I mean by this is that God will keep us from the ultimate evil. That ultimate evil is not death. If I were hit by a bomb or a shell . . . they who love me must not think of it as God's failure to keep me. To be kept by God means to be in His love whether living or dying, being hit or escaping. . . . The ultimate evil would be the absence of love. A life outside it would be more evil than a death in it. While we may not be delivered from evils, if God keeps us we shall be delivered from Evil."

When we grow afraid of life and death, let us have the sense of the trustworthiness of the universe, of its encompassing embrace and its sustaining care, and let us know that we can never travel beyond the arms of the Divine.

These are some of the truths about fear and worry. A certain amount of anxiety is normal to us all. We cannot help it in this time of separation of families, international tension, and economic and social uncertainty. The wisdom of life is "to endure what we must and to change what we can." Certain things we must endure, certain hardships and tragedies, defeats and losses, are part of our human destiny. We can master undue fear, however, when we learn to understand its origin in the soil of our childhood, when we take advantage of the resources, physical, medical, religious, and psychiatric, which can brush away the cobwebs from our souls, and when we come to accept ourselves with our abilities and our limitations, our joys and our depressions, universal brothers experiencing universal emotions.

We can master fear not only by understanding it and accepting ourselves; we can also master it through work—work which is the best sublimation for our rage and anger and the truest escape from self-pity and self-centeredness—work which gives us dignity and which will help to bring about a society where there will be food and security and freedom for all.

Finally, we master fear through faith—faith in the worthwhileness of life and the trustworthiness of God; faith in the meaning of our pain and our striving, the confidence that God will not cast us aside but will use each one of us as a piece of priceless mosaic in the design of His universe.

CHAPTER SIX

Grief's Slow Wisdom

R ELIGION throughout the ages has sought to give men both comfort and courage in the presence of death. Religion has approached this universal problem of human mortality in a variety of ways: sometimes it has attempted to imbue men with a stoical outlook upon the cessation of life; sometimes it has solaced the bereaved heart with the confident assurance of personal immortality beyond the shores of death, contrasting the ugliness and frustrations of earthly life with the ineffable bliss which God has laid up in heaven.

All religions have developed sacramental techniques for meeting the challenge of death, surrounding the end of life with the halo of sacred solemnity. Church and synagogue have created what might be called "strategies of solace" for these poignant hours when man walks through the valley of the shadow, strategies of solace built out of music and words—the intonation of liturgical hymns, the somber rendition of immortal psalms, the rehearsal of the virtues and the graces of the departed. Religious rituals at the time of death, no matter how much they may differ in form and in content, seek to perform two functions: to ferry the departed one safely across the waters of oblivion to the shores of eternity, and at the same time to build a bridge upon which the bereaved living can move from the numbness of sorrow toward a renewed acceptance of life.

In a sense, religion attempts its most heroic feat in the presence of the grave. It asserts, on the one hand, that the dead have passed from the painful experiences of this life either into blessed oblivion or into a realm of higher existence, transcendent and infinite. On the other hand, it summons the survivors, educated by tragedy, to accept anew the blessings and the burdens of earthly life.

Religion, in other words, often balances itself perilously over the abyss, like a juggler tossing his spheres in the air while traversing a tightrope. Church and synagogue, confronted with the ultimate mystery, must somehow do justice to these somewhat contradictory concepts—the tragic fragility of our brief day on earth and the reassertion of the value of that day in spite of its fragility. They must console the bereaved, but accomplish this purpose in such a way as not to congeal the life impulse in the living. When religion goes to the extreme, as it sometimes does, of deprecating this world and magnifying its imperfections, it implicitly encourages morbidity and pessimism, thereby diminishing the life hunger in the hearts of the living. At that point, religion itself becomes the ally of death, tending to transform men from healthy-mindedness to sick-mindedness.

Not that it is easy to resist negative and pessimistic thoughts when confronted by the passing of a loved one. Poets, novelists, and philosophers throughout the centuries have written their most somber and frightening lines when dealing with the menace of death. They grow bitter at the shears of fate which ruthlessly sever the thread of being. They draw vivid word portraits of the unbearable pain of separation, the unfairness of destiny which too frequently plunges its dagger into the pulsating bodies of lovers even as they drain the cup of ecstasy. Poets weep, and make us weep, at the fate of young lives cut short while senility stumbles meaninglessly along its blind highway. They rebel, and make us rebel, at the dark magic of the universe which in the twinkling of an eye can transform the breathing, laughing, creating artist, scientist, son, mother, wife, into a silent, unoccupied tenement of clay, a shroud of darkness, a crumbling clod of earth. Perhaps the very resentment which poets have expressed at the sovereignty of death is the supreme testimony of the hunger for life which resides in most men.

Whatever the explanation, it is undeniably true that literature, when dealing with death, has most frequently expressed not acquiescence, but revolt; not courage, but tears and sorrow. Incidentally, the most perfect proof of the finiteness of our minds may be derived from the fact that the writers of ancient Judea and Greece seem to have known as much about death as the most contemporary of poets; though the idiom and the verse form may be different, there is little essential distinction between what the writers of twenty centuries ago said on this ultimate problem and what the writers say about it today. We are all baffled children before the scythe of the grim reaper, and the themes which can be played to express our emotions or to articulate our thoughts are extremely limited in number. Their combination into new forms may be endless, but the basic motifs are identical: courage or cowardice, stoicism or self-pity, work or weeping.

Peace of Mind

It is, of course, not true that all religions have dealt with the problem of death in identical fashion. There are Oriental religions which base themselves upon the negation of life and the quest for surcease and nirvana. Some forms of Christianity have vacillated between the negation of life and its affirmation. Judaism in its major traditions has attempted to avoid morbidity and pessimism, and has rather consistently sought to give its followers a sane perspective about life and death, a courageous acceptance of the role of death in the economy of life, and a life-sustaining interest in this world in spite of tragedy and loss.

Religion customarily deals with grief and death in terms of faith and philosophy. It tries to bring solace through the presentation of a creed about immortality, personal and social. It attempts to persuade the mind and the heart to spiritual resignation, yet in dealing with the pain of bereavement, men need not only a spiritual faith, but an emotional strategy which will enable them to manage bereavement creatively rather than destructively. Men throughout the ages have tried to evolve a proper emotional technique for dealing with grief, and occasionally poets and philosophers intuitively arrived at wise solutions of this problem.

In general, however, there has been widespread confusion as to the right approach to take about grief. Should emotion be expressed or repressed? Should sorrow be verbalized or concealed? Should children be exposed to grief or should they be completely insulated from it? These questions concern one of the crucial and decisive areas of human life—the emotional reaction to final earthly separation. Answers to these questions are increasingly indispensable today since the war in-

Grief's Slow Wisdom

evitably has brought tragic news to countless homes. If men and women do not know how to face bereavement and adjust to it, no truly good life will be possible for this generation. I say that no good life will be possible because people pain-ridden in body, or neurotic in mind, are poor architects of the good life. And as we shall see, the unwise attitudes that people take to grief are now found to be the source of many medical diseases and psychic maladjustments.

Probably the leading pioneer in this area of the emotional life of man—an area rather neglected by psychiatrists in their absorption with the more obvious distortions of sex, hate, inferiority—is the distinguished Harvard psychiatrist, Dr. Erich Lindemann. In his clinical work at the Massachusetts General Hospital with hundreds of grief patients, he has uncovered some basic new truths about both normal and abnormal grief reactions. He has found, in the first place, that in cases where someone really important in the life pattern of the individual had died, the bereaved normally experienced these reactions for a period of several weeks or months: bodily symptoms of pain and distress, continual preoccupation with the image of the deceased, deep feelings of guilt, disinterestedness in life, and loss of patterns of conduct.

Almost every person who suffers a severe loss should expect these reactions in greater or less degree. If they are understood as temporary manifestations, if the bereaved person is wise enough to do his grief work courageously by accepting rather than avoiding intense feelings of sadness, by expressing his emotions rather than suppressing them, by readjusting to the environment bereft of the loved one, and by beginning to form new relationships—if these things are done, a true grief strategy has been discovered and the dangers of future neuroses averted.

However, a number of patients, Dr. Lindemann found, had repressed their real feeling of grief, and as a direct result of that repression many morbid reactions, sooner or later, made their appearance. Some people were living a life of rage and anger against the whole world without knowing why. Other patients had developed severe depressions years after the loss of the loved one, without an awareness of any connection between the present depression and the complete denial of grief at an earlier stage in their life history. Thirty-three out of forty-one patients with ulcerative colitis had developed their disease "in close time-relationship with the loss of an important person." Patients suffering from physical disease or from mental disturbance (whether that disturbance showed itself in complete withdrawal from social contact, in excessive aggressiveness, in agitated depression) were helped when the psychiatrist was able to make them open the floodgates of emotion, thus removing the barriers that they had set up against the expression of grief. In this way the morbid grief reaction was transformed into a normal grief pattern, and a new and healthy-minded adjustment to life usually ensued.

The brilliant research work of this psychiatrist indicates that various types of neuroses and physical diseases can be traced back to the bereavement experience, immediate or remote, in the life history of men and women. These individuals sternly had repressed their grief, and that repression was the major source of their present disturbance. When the patient was induced to relive the emotion that he felt at the time of his bereavement, and to express unrestrainedly the genuine

Grief's Slow Wisdom

sorrow and heartache which he should have expressed at the time of the death of the loved one, the re-enacted bereavement was his emotional release from bondage, a genuine catharsis of the soul. Amazing cures resulted when patients were persuaded to express the pain and sorrow that should normally have been given outlet at the time of the funeral, and in the period directly following the great loss.

Dynamic psychology, in other words, is now able to aid religion in its struggle against human misery and unhappiness, both among adults and children. While it may be true that there is little new that may be said on the subject of death itself, much that is new may be said on the subject of our attitude toward death. I find in Dr. Lindemann's clinical investigations many important implications for religion as it deals with the problem of grief. Naturally, the scientist is interested primarily in giving us the facts about normal and abnormal grief; it is for us to interpret those facts in the light of religious experience and human need.

We must safeguard ourselves, of course, against any unwarranted generalizations. There are many different temperaments among men; some are more phlegmatic than others; their stoicism is but a reflection of their glandular constitution. Other people are abnormally sensitive and feel with acute pain every slight disappointment and rebuff which life may mete out to them. Some individuals are tough-minded and others are tender-minded; in short, there is a temperamental chasm which separates these categories of human personality. Furthermore, the sudden death of a laughing child or a promising youth will normally produce paroxysms of sorrow whereas the passing of an old grandmother who long since has outlived her own desire for existence will be greeted with far greater calm and acquiescence. We must understand, then, that there is almost an infinite gamut of emotional reactions which divergent human personalities may manifest in the presence of death. Occasionally no real grief is felt; sometimes grief is felt and expressed, but is mastered by a strong, well-integrated personality. Sometimes grief is felt and remains unexpressed and comes to master and dominate the whole personality. It is this latter state that is most harmful and therefore to be avoided.

Three Laws for Governing Grief

Let us analyze a typical grief situation, and through this analysis formulate some laws of psychic health. When a person suffers the loss of a beloved with whom there have been vital interpersonal relations, the immediate result is a terrible inner numbness and a loss of equilibrium; a feeling that one has no longer any conduct patterns to follow. The world is a dreary wasteland. Grief, loneliness, despair possess his soul. Shall he give way to these passions, or eternally crush them down?

One of the greatest illusions about human nature is that the expression of grief will lead to a breakdown. *Quite the reverse.* No one has ever broken down nervously through the legitimate expression of an emotional reaction. The distortion, the concealment, the denial of our normal human feelings may well prove the breeding ground of delayed breakdowns. The truth is that we human beings are tough organisms and can withstand much rough handling. How absurd is

Grief's Slow Wisdom

that notion current in modern society that men and women must be safeguarded, coddled, and shielded against emotional outbursts. It is not those outbursts which harm the human organism, but the complete avoidance of them, which scars and tears the fabric of the inner soul.

The first law, then, which should be followed in the time of the loss of a loved one is: *express as much grief as you actually feel.* Do not be ashamed of your emotions. Do not be afraid of breaking down under the strain of your loss. The pain that you feel now will be the tool and the instrument of your later healing. Furthermore, the function of friends is to be the sounding board for the grief of the bereaved. Instead of trying to distract attention from the loss—a procedure that should come much later in the healing process—friends should offer the opportunity and encouragement to the man who has lost a loved one, to talk about his loss, to dwell upon his sorrow, and to rehearse the beauty and the virtues of the departed one.

A second new truth about the grief situation is this: *we must learn how to extricate ourselves from the bondage of the physical existence and coexistence of the loved one.* A husband and wife who have lived and worked together harmoniously, sharing with each other the successes and failures of the common struggle, inevitably build their hopes upon the assumption of the continuity of the marital pattern. The death of one of the partners leaves an aching void and a gaping hole in the fabric of life. Death comes quickly, but it cannot quickly erase the expectancies of a lifetime from the slate of memory and the surviving partner yearns in vain for the presence of the comrade. The achievement of mental balance will be expedited if the pain of loneliness and loss will be courageously accepted

113

and lived through rather than evaded and avoided. Words have their own magic potency, and human speech has the most blessed ability to compound balm and medicine for the overburdened heart. It is only by speaking to others of the loss and of the magnitude of that bereavement that gradually the pain itself proves bearable.

We are, in a deep sense, what our relationships to other human beings make us. You know that you become gay in the presence of the gay, you are stimulated to thought in the presence of the intellectual, you see something of the majesty of art when in the presence of a fine painter. We are like great mines filled with rich ore, waiting to be discovered and brought to the surface of the earth.

We all of us have different capacities and powers waiting for the appropriate miner, some friend, some comrade, some loved one who will explore and bring the shining metal of our hearts, our minds, our talents to the surface of reality. Too many people make the mistake, however, in hours of bereavement, of closing the door to the mines of their spirits and permitting no entrance to new friends and comrades who could bring up much precious ore. These grief-stricken lives become abandoned mines with all of the unused shafts covered with the cobwebs of self-pity.

The melody that the loved one played upon the piano of our life will never be played quite that way again, but we must not close the keyboard and allow the instrument to gather dust. We must seek out other artists of the spirit, new friends who gradually will help us to find the road to life again, who will walk on that road with us. The establishment of new patterns of interaction with other people, beginning with the in-

teraction of language and moving on to new avenues of creative expression, is the second law for the conquest of grief and
the conquest of death.

A third law may be expressed as follows: *when death destroys an important relationship, it is essential that someone
be found partially capable of replacing that relationship.* Equilibrium will be restored when the bereaved person discovers
some situation demanding the same or similar patterns of conduct. For example, a mother who loses a young child has suffered one of the most tragic bereavements of all, particularly
because often the mother and the child have not yet become
separate personalities. The mother feels literally as though she
had lost an eye or a limb—a part of her very being. Now, when
such a tragedy occurs, that love pattern must be re-established
in some way. What can be done to bring into play this law of
pattern replacement? A mother after the death of her own
child should be encouraged, for example, to interest herself in
daily work at a nursery school. She should be stimulated by the
minister or the psychologist to transfer the conduct pattern
which she had fashioned in her relationship with her own child
into work with a group of children.

It would be unwise for this mother to adopt a baby immediately, because unconsciously she would feel disloyal to her
own dead child in this speedy transference of love to a
stranger. The adopted child in turn would become the unconscious victim of a deep hostility. A very wise solution occurs
if the bereaved mother dilutes her affection at first over a wide
area in working with the nursery-school children. Then, when
the first deep wound has partially healed, she either adopts a
child or has one of her own and bestows upon it her mature

and devoted affection. This illustration is merely a symbol of the procedure that must be followed where a truly great loss has occurred; namely, the procedure of displacement and of replacement, the discovery of a new pattern of conduct similar to the one that has been broken by the intrusion of death.

We must face grief without any expectation of miraculous healing, but with the knowledge that if we are courageous and resolute we can live as our loved ones would wish us to live, not empty, morose, self-centered, and self-pitying, but as brave and undismayed servants of the greater life. Rabbinic wisdom teaches this approach to grief in the following passage: "When the second Temple in Jerusalem was destroyed many Jews began to withdraw from life and sank into a state of depressed mourning for the sons and daughters of Israel that had perished and also for the Temple that had gone up in smoke. They refused to eat and to drink." Rabbi Joshua said to them: "My sons, I know that it is impossible not to mourn, but to mourn excessively is forbidden." Why? Because that great Jewish sage felt that we human beings must think not only of the past but of the future. We are commanded by our religion to be the servants of life as long as we live.

It is this wisdom that we must take to heart today. If a dear one has passed away, an invalid to whose welfare we have been devoted for years, then we must find some other person or persons in need of our loving care, and that very devotion which we lavish on life will be the substitute therapy, the miraculous healing that will come to our torn spirits. If it is a son or a brother or a husband who has died in the battle for freedom, then our grief must be transmuted into the work for the unfinished cause which he left behind. We must act as the ambassadors of our departed, their messengers and their spokesmen, carrying out the mission for which they lived and strove and which they bequeathed to us. They lived, they toiled, they laughed, they served, and we must be their worthy emissaries in the portion of life that they leave behind them.

We have seen thus far that when a person suffers a really tragic loss, he will be aided in his future adjustment to life, first by expressing rather than repressing his grief, and secondly by having relatives or friends aid him to find some parallel pattern of action, some new area of life interest, which will serve as a substitute for the pattern which death has annihilated. It must be recognized, of course, that these substitute patterns of life will not come spontaneously and without effort. The mourner must inevitably live through many lonely hours and empty days, often despairing of any recovery of an interest in human affairs again. Even in normal grief there is no real short cut to readjustment and renewed life interest.

Up to this point I have been describing laws for psychic health which apply primarily to normal men and women who have achieved emotional maturity long before the tragedy of death occurred, expressing that maturity in the integrated character of their love relationships. It will be more difficult to apply these laws about grief to men and women whose emotional lives either are immature or are corroded with unresolved aggressions. It is hard to help a person move from a morbid to a healthy grief state if he has been involved in some undesirable or unhealthy emotional relationship with the deceased. When, for example, a son has devoted his life to his mother and has really never been emancipated from her, the mother's death will leave him at such loose ends that he may spend the rest of his days in an emotional vacuum. He has really never freed himself from a dependency upon his mother, and her going may be such a traumatic shock that he too perishes spiritually, although he may continue to breathe and to act physically.

To grieve to death because of a bereavement is a much rarer occurrence than literature would have us imagine. "Men have died . . . and worms have eaten them, but not for love," says Shakespeare. But there are innumerable instances of men and women whose love for the lost one has been of a passive, dependent nature, rather than of a mature mutuality. An unrelenting melancholia which continues for years may in rare instances be the sign of a love more precious than the world itself, but more often such melancholia is an indication that the love relationship was a counterfeit, another name for dependent attachment to a magic helper now vanished. If a person continues to mourn his dear one without any realistic concern for the rest of human life and the tasks waiting to be done, he reveals a kind of inadequacy in his love: he proves that he never really became a mature, self-reliant individual. Such a person transforms the earth into a funeral home, hearing no other voice save his own raised in self-pity. Difficult as it may be to believe at first, the mourning of certain men and women is really a mourning for themselves, an expression of self-centered pity for their own directionless lives. One of the most arduous tasks for both the psychologist and the religious teacher is to help a person who was immature in his attachment before the death of the loved one gradually to achieve emotional adulthood.

I recently came across a striking illustration of morbid grief

Grief's Slow Wisdom

and emotional suicide in reading the poem of Robert Frost
called *Home Burial*. The poet describes the mood of a grief-
stricken mother who refuses to accept life and the love of her
husband and makes a shrine out of her own sorrow. Fum-
blingly the husband tries to open a door into his wife's grief.
He pleads with her to take up the threads of life again:

> *Let me into your grief . . .*
> *I do think though you overdo it a little.*
> *What was it brought you up to think it the thing*
> *To take your mother-loss of a first child*
> *So inconsolably—in the face of love?*

The mother wilfully refuses to conquer her grief; she deter-
mines to make sorrow her way of life. In bitterness she says to
her husband:

> *Friends make pretence of following to the grave,*
> *But before one is in it, their minds are turned*
> *And making the best of their way back to life*
> *And living people, and things they understand.*
> *But the world's evil. I won't have grief so*
> *If I can change it. Oh, I won't, I won't!*

Another little-recognized source of psychic anxiety that
manifests itself after the death of a loved one are the guilt feelings which are subtly allied with the feelings of unresolved
hostility toward the departed. Few people recognize how
often their emotions are mixed, how inevitably there is a tinc-
ture of anger even in the purest love. Education and religion
conspire to make us feel ashamed of our normal aggressive
impulses; some people go throughout their lives never admit-

119

Peace of Mind

ting to themselves any moods of hatred or resentment toward their loved ones. Social convention makes hypocrites out of multitudes, and, what is worse, unconscious hypocrites at that.

A daughter, for example, hypnotized by the moral precepts that she has heard all her life, feels compelled to love her mother, even though that mother may always have taken advantage of the daughter, made a slavey out of her, a servant of her tyrannical whims. Society has ordained that the child must "honor the parent," and therefore that daughter has accepted subservient devotion on her part as an inescapable axiom of her life. The mother dies. Some time later the daughter develops a severe neurosis. To the casual observer it might seem that she has grown ill because she is reproaching herself for some minor failures or shortcomings in her care of her mother. The real explanation is that hidden very deeply in the unconscious of that daughter is a bitter resentment against the mother which she has concealed even from herself. She seems to grieve because of the loss of her mother, but part of her grief comes because now she can never express toward her mother the rage that she really has felt.

In one degree or another, this process takes place with countless individuals. They have never admitted to themselves the true nature of their relationship to parent or to husband. They have lived a lie psychologically, completely unaware of the truth that all love is a compound in which some elements of anger and aggression are intermingled. Since they have never been able to admit even to themselves the presence of normal hostility at certain moments in their love relationship, they overindulge in morbid guilt feelings now that the final separation has occurred. They can no longer express any

120

of that aggression toward the one who has died and therefore they turn it inward upon themselves! Out of that imprisoned unconscious hostility the deep sickness of their soul is born. It becomes almost impossible even to verbalize the latent anger, since here, too, society has trained us to speak only good of the dead, to magnify the virtues of the departed one, and to pass over in silence his inadequacies and defects. When a person grows morbid, apparently out of grief, and continually indulges in self-recrimination at some supposed failure or unimportant quarrel, we ought to suspect that both the grief and the guilt feelings are façades behind which lurks the real cause of the disturbance: an unacknowledged rebellion and resentment repressed during all of the life of the father, mother, or husband.

What can be done to cure such a person?

Religion has provided some wise outlets as forms of expiation for these guilt feelings. It has assured the worshiper that God will forgive the unconfessed sin, provided proper atonement is made and sacrificial deeds are performed. Bequests to charity and lavish gifts to religious institutions after the death of a member of a family may serve as therapeutic devices whereby the bereaved atone by acts of sacrifice for their inner aggressions.

Modern psychology probably would add another strategy of expression as an escape from morbid guilt feelings; it would suggest some violent physical exertion as an outlet for pent-up emotions, in the conviction that outer activity, strenuous and athletic, is far preferable to inner self-mutilation, the turning of unspent aggression against oneself. The modern religious counselor trained in psychology should also try to persuade the grieving person that a measure of anger resides in every experience of love. When once a man has been made to see that nothing human is perfect, and that it is quite normal for everyone to experience moods of resentment and of hostility even toward the most beloved parent, brother, or comrade, then the needless burden of guilt is lifted like a cloud which too long has darkened the horizon of life, and the mourner is liberated from the oppression of guilty grief.

The discoveries of psychiatry—of how essential it is to express rather than to repress grief, to talk about one's loss with friends and companions, to move step by step from inactivity to activity again—remind us that the ancient teachers of Judaism often had an intuitive wisdom about human nature and its needs which our more sophisticated and liberal age has forgotten. Traditional Judaism, as a matter of fact, had the wisdom to devise almost all of the procedures for healthy-minded grief which the contemporary psychologist counsels, although Judaism naturally did not possess the tools for scientific experiment and systematic case study, nor did it always understand, as we now can, the underlying reason for its procedures. The Bible records how open and unashamed was the expression of sorrow on the part of Abraham and Jacob and David. Our ancestors publicly wept, wore sackcloth, tore their garments, and fasted. In rabbinic literature we read that "The time of mourning is divided into four periods. The first three days are given to weeping and lamentation; the deceased is eulogized up to the seventh day, the mourner keeping within the house; the somber garb of mourning is worn up to the thirtieth day, and personal adornment is neglected. In the case

122

of mourning for a parent, the pursuit of amusement and entertainment is abandoned up to the end of the year. . . ."

On returning from the burial, *shiva* commences—the seven days during which the mourner is confined to the house in which he sits on the floor or on a low bench, devoting his time to the reading of the book of Job. The first meal after the funeral is prepared by a neighbor and is called "the meal of consolation." Friends and neighbors and relatives come to visit the mourner, and the conversation is limited to the praises of the deceased.

The ancient Jews thus arranged for the expression of grief and stimulated that expression by ordaining wailing, the tearing of the garment, the repetition of the tearstained pages of the Bible—the creation of an unashamed atmosphere of sorrow. Furthermore, the rabbis prescribed that the conversation in the house of mourning should revolve around the dead person, thus providing the mourner an opportunity to articulate his sense of loss. In the famous ethical work *The Sayings of the Fathers,* we come across the advice of one of the great rabbinic sages, Rabbi Simeon ben Eleazar, who said "Seek not to comfort thy neighbor while his dead still lies before him. . . ." Note, furthermore, how traditional Judaism arranged a kind of hierarchical order in the process of mourning: the first days after the burial being the period of most intense mourning, with a gradual tapering off of that intensity of grief, by well-arranged time steps—seven days, thirty days, one year.

Where traditional Judaism was psychologically sound in its approach to death, much liberal religion has been unsound. We moderns have assimilated from our environment a sense of shame about emotionalism and a disinclination to face the tragic realities of life, both leading to unwise repression and emotional evasion. Liberal rabbis and liberal ministers alike are continually committing psychological fallacies. They arrange funerals in such a way as to make death itself almost an illusion. Often the ritual itself is planned in such a way as to prevent tears, emotional outbursts, and "undignified scenes." Even at the grave, the conspiracy of illusion is maintained. The coffin is hidden beneath a blanket of flowers and the brown earth is concealed by an artificial carpet of green. All this is done, no doubt, with the best of intentions, with the desire of sparing the feelings and of shielding the bereaved from possible paroxysms of grief. The same noble motive animates the friends and relatives of the mourners when they attempt to distract attention from the poignant loss, employing all kinds of conversational devices to divert the mind of the bereaved. Startling though it may seem at first, all this is wrong. It proceeds on the assumption that men should not give in to themselves; that indulgence in emotion is harmful; that the bereaved must be protected against despairing thoughts; that the tragic realities of life should be glossed over and avoided. This approach is a reflection of our whole twentieth century's suspicion of emotion, when the expression of honest feeling has become so taboo.

The whole superficiality of modern civilization is revealed in one sense in this realm of the grief situation. Modern man has made a god out of comfort and has grown afraid of facing reality in all of its depths. We live in an age when the machines of our invention tend to atrophy some of our muscles. We also live in an age when out of our desire to avoid the unpleasant

Grief's Slow Wisdom

and to hide the painful from our eyes we have been in danger likewise of permitting the atrophy of our emotions. One of the greatest discoveries of Sigmund Freud was that emotions denied their proper expression in life do not really disappear; they live on in a submerged fashion and create the dynamite of psychic conflict and misery. Unexpressed emotions ultimately have their vengeance in the form of mental and physical illness. Now, many people tend to think that this truth about the emotional life applies only to the area of our sexual impulses. The experiments of Dr. Lindemann dealing with the emotion of grief indicate that there is a universal necessity for the legitimate expression of our feelings in every dimension of life, and that the unwise repression of any emotion leads all too frequently to frustration and maladjustment.

The conclusion, then, of the newest psychological research is that when we face the loss of a dear one, we should allow our hearts full leeway in the expression of their pain. We should not pretend to grieve when we do not feel it, when, for example, an aged parent who has been suffering from an incurable disease is given surcease by death. On the other hand, we must not be afraid to articulate the wildness of our sorrow if that is what we genuinely feel. We must never falsify our emotions in conformity with conventions. Nor should we prematurely seek for speedy comfort and consolation. Let us understand that the experience of pain somehow has a curative function and that any evasive detour around normal sorrow will bring us later to a tragic abyss. After all, we were given tear ducts to use just for such hours of darkness. Not only should we be unashamed of grief, confident that its expression will not permanently hurt us, but we should also possess the wisdom to talk about our loss and through that creative conversation with friends and companions begin to reconstruct the broken fragments of our lives.

We should not resist the sympathy and the stimulation of social interaction. We should learn not to grow impatient with the slow healing process of time. We should discipline ourselves to recognize that there are many steps to be taken along the highway leading from sorrow to renewed serenity and that it is folly to attempt prematurely to telescope and compress these successive stages of recuperation into a miraculous cure. We should not demand of ourselves more than nature herself will permit. We should anticipate these stages in our emotional convalescence: unbearable pain, poignant grief, empty days, resistance to consolation, disinterestedness in life, gradually giving way under the healing sunlight of love, friendship, social challenge, to the new weaving of a pattern of action and the acceptance of the irresistible challenge of life.

Life is distorted not merely for adults, but for children, when the grief situation is unwisely handled. There is more human misery prevalent in the world because of the fallacious approach that adults take to children on the death problem than we would ever imagine. This is what frequently happens. A father dies, leaving a young child and a widow. At the time of the funeral the little boy is sent to some strange relative and the widowed mother and all the relatives conspire to conceal from the child the true situation. The father's name is not mentioned or, if mentioned, the conversation is quickly turned to some other channel. The theory behind all this conspiracy of silence about the death of the father is that the little boy should be shielded from grief and pain. "He is too young to know the truth." This whole process of concealment, while motivated by the highest intentions, can prove to be terribly distorting to the child's emotional development.

This is not theoretical speculation on my part. I recently learned of several case studies which definitely prove the danger of dishonesty and falsehood in any dealings with children, but particularly in so important an area as that of grief and death. Two young boys, four and five years of age respectively, lost their father. The mother, a very disciplined and undemonstrative person who regarded emotional scenes as violations of the social code of conduct, sent the two little boys to an aunt so that they would be out of the house during the funeral services. After three weeks the little boys returned to their home. No mention was made of the father. When they inquired about him, they were told he had gone away and that they should ask no further questions.

The boys, prevented from obtaining any satisfaction about the disappearance of their father, began to imagine many things and soon came to this terrifying conclusion: their mother had killed their father and had hidden his body somewhere! They never confided this frightening thought to anyone else, but grew up with this ghost in their minds. All throughout childhood and adolescence the brothers were so haunted by the fantasy of their mother as a murderess that they developed deep-seated phobias, the older brother imagining himself condemned to become a murderer, and the younger brother always picturing himself in the role of the murdered. In their early twenties these two brothers, having developed completely neurotic personalities, were forced to undergo prolonged psychiatric treatment and were cured only when the early source of their mental distortions was found in the un-wise handling of the original bereavement situation.

An even more striking and unfortunately more tragic case recently came to my attention. A young girl of seventeen was brought to a hospital, suffering from severe ulcerative colitis. There was no known organic reason for this disease which had wasted her body. Scientific investigation uncovered this re-markable story. When this girl was three years of age her mother died as the result of an abortion. The little girl simply adored her mother and had made a complete identification with her. Everything the mother did the daughter imitated. Immediately after the death of the mother the little girl was sent away, and when she returned she found a house of bitter-ness. The mother's name was not mentioned and the grand-parents treated her beloved father as though he were a crimi-nal; several times when they thought the child was not within hearing distance, they called the father a murderer. The little girl became the innocent victim of the battle between the father and the grandparents. All that she knew was that her beloved mother was gone. Nobody told her where she had gone, but from whispers and hints and sentences broken off in the middle, from bitter glances and angry gestures, she came to the conclusion that her mother had done something wrong with her stomach, had been an evil person, and was punished in her stomach because of that evil.

The three-year-old child then developed by identification with the mother a severe case of stomach trouble. This appar-ently was cured, but the child never was able to establish any clear image of her mother or any permanently satisfying rela-tionship with her father. She wanted to love him, but she was

Grief's Slow Wisdom

prevented from that love by the remembrance of the whispered accusations of the grandparents that her father was a murderer. Her emotional life became completely entangled, and in early adolescence, under the stress and strain of physical and mental tension, she collapsed and died.

What should have been done in this case? The little girl should have been told that the mother had died because of an accident, a mistake that she had made. The story of that mistake and of the sorrow and anger of the grandparents could have been told the little girl by her father—told, naturally, on the child's level of comprehension. If she had been taken into her father's confidence and if he instead of ruthlessly repressing his own feelings had broken down and cried with the girl, a new pattern of comradeship would have been established and the child would have had one sure ally in her battle for growth and normal maturity. She could have adjusted to the truth about her mother, her father, and her grandparents if the adult world had been wise enough to realize that children, even the youngest of them, can stand tragedy, sorrow, tears, much better than they can stand lies, deceit, evasions.

I know that these cases sound fantastic. At first it will be hard to believe that a three-year-old girl or a five-year-old boy can be affected ten or twenty years later by a long-forgotten grief episode. Yet this is the brilliant revelation of Freud that the events of early childhood prove to be the decisive traumas in life. What happens in the first few years of existence has fractured many a soul.

In my pastoral work not long ago I had occasion to see this truth in action. A man lost his father and was prostrate with grief. The mother had sent their seven-year-old girl to a distant relative without explanation. The child knew something was wrong, since this was the first time she had ever been separated from her father and mother. She also knew that her father was not now the laughing, gay person he always had been.

When I asked about the little girl, the father and mother told me what they had done, asking me whether I did not agree with the wisdom of their procedure. "You know, we are only doing this for her sake. She is too young to be around this house with all the sorrow." I told the parents that they were, in my judgment, doing their child a great injustice, that she should be brought home immediately, told briefly that her grandfather had died and that her father needed her to cheer him up and to make him forget his loss. She should be given an important function to perform, namely, to "mother" and comfort her father.

The parents followed this counsel, the little girl returned, forced her father to sit down on the floor and play with her, and both she and her father were drawn infinitely closer together by the mutuality of their experience. The parents did discover that their daughter had felt terribly rejected during her separation from them and already was beginning to fill her vivid imagination with frightening thoughts of desertion and loneliness.

Now, I do not mean to imply that children have to be told the details about death. No long or involved discussion about the mystery of the grave and what lies beyond is ever necessary with young children. The story of life and death must be told on their level of comprehension and in their child's frame of reference. The adult world should shield the child from the grotesque and horrifying aspects of death when such are pres-

Grief's Slow Wisdom

ent. A child's mind should never be needlessly frightened. All this is true, but what is a supreme illusion among men is the idea that children cannot stand grief and sadness, that under all circumstances they must be coddled and sheltered against the winds of reality. No, the truth lies in exactly the opposite direction. The child can stand tears but not treachery, sorrow but not deceit. The little boy or girl should be dealt with in a straightforward, honest fashion; he should be allowed to share and participate in the family's woes as well as triumphs. The little organism is much tougher than we sometimes think. It will not dissolve in a little salt water shed by the childish eye. It will not break under honestly presented grief. It may break under the burden of exclusion and exile from the family circle, under the heavy load of adult evasion, half-truths, frozen emotions, hypocritical pretenses.

I have dwelt at length on the subject of grief as it should be experienced both by adults and by children because the theme itself is so vital in this warring age and because the whole grief process verifies the religious intuition that this is a truth-demanding universe. Lies are boomerangs.

This world is so made that we have to respect truth. What we have learned scientifically about the whole bereavement situation vividly demonstrates that when we, as adults, lie to ourselves about our own emotions by suppressing our feelings of grief, burying them deep in the subvault of our unconscious, then the universe wreaks havoc with our emotional life for this violation of truth. The whole grief process proves that psychic happiness and serenity are dependent upon the honesty which we show to others and the honesty we show to ourselves. Life commands us, "Be true to your own feelings rather than to outer conventions. Be true also in all of your interpersonal relationships with young and old alike. Be confident of your own strength to withstand the shocks and tragedies of life and know that the universe, which demands truth, has within it the powers for your healing. The world wounds, but it also miraculously distills medicine and balm for those wounds. Trust life, face it without mask or masquerade, and you will yet conquer sorrow and be victorious over grief."

For those who have lost loved ones during the tragic war, all of the rest of life will be but a half loaf of bread—yet a half loaf eaten in courage and accepted in truth is infinitely better than a moldy whole loaf, green with the decay of self-pity and selfish sorrow which really dishonors the memory of those who lived for our upbuilding and happiness.

Perhaps it is all a matter of compensation. Just as the man who loses the use of one of his senses develops unusual keenness in another sense organ as part of life's compensatory scheme, so we in seeking out and in establishing new interests and new friendships will compensate for the loss we have grievously suffered. This is perhaps the greatest blessing that God has given man—the ability to build new bridges of human companionship until the day that we die. This blessing, the ability to make new friends, is not only reserved for youth but is one that we can exercise in maturity and in old age. As long as we live, we never lose the power to weave new patterns of interpersonal relationships and to make ourselves richer, more creative, more interesting, and more interested characters.

There can be no profound human life without its measure of sorrow, but as religion, aided by the new insights of dynamic psychology, teaches modern man how to face grief and transcend it, many of the neurotic mysteries of our day will be solved, many of the emotional maladjustments which torment children and adults will disappear. Tutored by "grief's slow wisdom," the human family will surmount the hill of tragedy and descend into the valley of inner peace.

CHAPTER SEVEN

Intimations of Our Immortality

IT is not often that we are brave enough to come face to face with the thought of our own mortality. We make a tortuous, fearful approach to the dark cliff where death sits in wait for us. Yet as V. A. Koskeniemi has said, "Man is not free in life unless he is free from the fear of death too. We can certainly not be rid of it by not thinking of death, but on the contrary only by becoming accustomed to it, by learning to be at home in it. Thus we snatch from it its greatest advantage over us, its strangeness. In preparing ourselves for death, we prepare ourselves for freedom, and only he who has learned to die is free from life's slavery...."

As far as our own deaths are concerned, we should remember what science teaches about the process of dying. Men needlessly frighten themselves with anticipated horrors which never come to pass. As the famous physician, Sir William Osler, put it, "Most human beings not only die like heroes, but in my wide, clinical experience, die really without pain or fear. There is as much oblivion about the last hours as about the first, and therefore men fill their minds with specters that have no reality."

Montaigne said some wonderfully wise things about this very problem. "Nature herself gives us courage," he said.

Intimations of Our Immortality

"When I have been in perfect health, I have been much more afraid of sickness than when I have really felt the sickness." So shall it be with death. . . . If you have lived one day you have seen all. One day is equal to all other days. There is no other light; there is no other night. Death is not to be feared. It is a friend. Moreover, no man dies before his hour. The time you leave behind was no more yours than that which was before your birth and concerneth you no more. Make room for others as others have done for you. Like a full-fed guest, depart to rest. . . . The profit of life consists not in the space but rather in the use. Some man hath lived long that has had a short life. . . . Depart then without fear out of this world even as you came into it. The same way you came from death to life, return from life to death. Yield your torch to others as in a race. Your death is but a piece of the world's order, but a parcel of the world's life.

I often feel that death is not the enemy of life, but its friend, for it is the knowledge that our years are limited which makes them so precious. It is the truth that time is but lent to us which makes us, at our best, look upon our years as a trust handed into our temporary keeping. We are like children privileged to spend a day in a great park, a park filled with many gardens and playgrounds and azure-tinted lakes with white boats sailing upon the tranquil waves. True, the day allotted to each one of us is not the same in length, in light, in beauty. Some children of earth are privileged to spend a long and sunlit day in the garden of the earth. For others the day is shorter, cloudier, and dusk descends more quickly as in a winter's tale. But whether our life is a long summery day or a shorter wintry afternoon, we know that inevitably there are storms and squalls which overcast even the bluest heaven and there are sunlit rays which pierce the darkest autumn sky. The day that we are privileged to spend in the great park of life is not the same for all human beings, but there is enough beauty and joy and gaiety in the hours if we will but treasure them. Then for each one of us the moment comes when the great nurse, death, takes man, the child, by the hand and quietly says, "It is time to go home. Night is coming. It is your bedtime, child of earth. Come; you're tired. Lie down at last in the quiet nursery of nature and sleep. Sleep well. The day is gone. Stars shine in the canopy of eternity."

The presence of death makes more meaningful all of the values of life. It is the teacher making us aware of the fragility and the nobility of the human dream. The younger and the more immature we are, the more difficult it is to accept the thought of an end to earthly experience. In our rebellious moments we feel that if we had designed the universe, we would have given man an ever-renewable fountain of youth, so that death could never come and the end of life could never be felt. Yet when we analyze this feeling, we realize that this is the petulant, unreflective desire of a distraught child. For, actually, would we wish to be bound eternally to the wheel of existence, knowing no surcease, finding no possibility of escape for sleep and eternal rest? Do we wish to be always up and doing? Would we want to live through a thousand years, ten thousand years of change and struggle, revolution and pain, conflict and labor?

Plato was right when he declared that infinite life on this earth for us human beings, even if it were possible, would not be desirable, for a never-ending existence would be without

Intimations of Our Immortality

heights or depths, without crescendo or diminuendo, without challenge or achievement. It would be a life of ennui, of boredom, of monotony. Louis Untermeyer in a poem about Heine puts into the mouth of the dying poet:

> *To be eternal—to vegetate through all eternity—*
> *No such everlastingness for me!*
> *God, if He can, keep me from such a blight.*

In a deep sense, it is an ineffable boon that the bright rays of the sun do not beat down on us forever, but that the twilight hour comes with its cool peace and its embracing rest. It is profoundly true that the joy of our striving and the zest of our aspirations, so precious because of their fragile contingency, would vanish if earthly immortality were our inescapable lot and destiny.

In fact, the more mature we grow, the more we recognize unsuspected wisdom in the way that nature arranges things; we discover strange harmonies and a fitting appropriateness in the distribution of energies at every stage in life and the waning of ardent intensities in the sunset years, so that the twilight comes often to a not-too-resistant heart. Apparently, nature does not have the power to create such marvelously sensitive organisms as we human beings are, and at the same time arrange for the durability in us of stone or mountain. This is a universe where everything has a price, and we cannot expect to purchase the fragile beauty of love and consciousness without the suffering of transciency and decay. Some men, intuitively aware of the fragility of human life, have tried to ape the stone by becoming as indifferent and callous, as uninvolved with feeling as possible. The Buddhist thought that life's pains and sorrows could be avoided by giving no hostages to fortune, by making no commitments to other human beings, showing no love, no tenderness. "Make thou, in all of the world, nothing dear to thee." This is a cure that is worse than the disease, for the glory of life consists in our very ability to feel deeply and experience widely; it is the part of wisdom to taste of the cup of joy and sorrow without inner rebelliousness, to accept with equanimity the inevitable fact that we and all we possess are transient just because we are such sensitive creatures; that the marvel of our make-up, the superb intricacy of our chemical, physical, spiritual organization, gives us our supreme blessings and makes our little day on earth infinitely more significant than all of the rocks and stones which last unchanged but also untouched by the winds of the centuries.

At the same time, when we attempt to fashion a philosophy for ourselves with which to confront the inevitability of our own death, we dare not ignore the hunger in the human heart for some kind of existence beyond this narrow span of life. Even such a realistic philosopher as William James, who had long been disinterested in the question of immortality, in the last few years of his life began to believe in its possibility. When asked why, he said, "Because I am just becoming fit to live." There is an almost universal feeling that God could not shut the door completely upon so many slowly developed talents and gifts, but that there must be infinite realms where man can use the powers he has achieved here in order to paint vaster portraits and sing nobler songs beyond the shores of mortality.

It is true that no traveler has ever returned from the bourne

Intimations of Our Immortality

of eternity and that the yearning for immortality may be merely a projection of the life instinct and the hunger for survival in the human heart. Yet, one should not lightly deny or dismiss the thoughts of the philosophers who insist that this is a creative universe and that there is nothing inherently irrational, illogical, or impossible about life in undreamed dimensions; that just as our present senses are incapable of visualizing with the naked eye the infra-red and the ultra-violet rays, so a creative, growing universe might well have hidden unsuspected continents beyond the perception of flesh and blood.

Many great thinkers, among them Plato, Kant, Tolstoy, insist that the very reasonableness of the world demands immortality, that nature could not have placed mind in man like a candle to be gutted in a passing wind. The human soul is not a bit player, condemned to say one brief line upon the stage of time and then make a final exit. The Divine Playwright surely could not have written His drama so poorly—prepared all the resplendent scenery of the earth as a prelude to the appearance of the hero, Man, only to permit him the stammering sentence of a brief moment of time—this life—and then make both him and the drama of existence ludicrous by eternal silence. Say the thinkers, this earth is but the prologue and many a rich act has been prepared for man in other worlds. Reason demands it, and morality cries out that our human strivings for justice, for love, for peace, require some eternal denouement, some immortal stage upon which all the perplexities and inequities of the prologue shall be solved and human destiny find both reconciliation and fulfillment.

Whether one agrees or disagrees with these speculative ar-

Peace of Mind

guments in behalf of life beyond the grave, one should always remember that there are other forms of immortality besides personal survival. Man perhaps displays his most remarkable and his most unselfish genius when he turns from the thought of individual immortality and finds strength and inspiration in the immortality of the human race, when he transfers his allegiance from his own small ego to mankind as a whole. Man at that moment transcends himself; his own life becomes significant as one link in the magnetic chain of humanity. The more we concentrate upon the immortality of mankind, strangely enough, the richer becomes our own individual life. As we link ourselves to all of the heroes and sages and martyrs, to all of the poets and thinkers of every race and every clime, we become part of a great and moving drama. We find along the road of the ages so many good companions. It is the miracle of our intellect that we are enabled to leap over space and ignore time and link ourselves in imagination with all of the master builders of civilization and culture everywhere. We share, then, in the immortality of mankind as a whole as we come to identify ourselves with the wisest thoughts, the noblest ideals, the richest music of the centuries. Poor, indeed, is the man who lives only in his own time. His life is thin and shadowy and at the mercy of every wind that blows. When he dies, too little dies with him. Rich, indeed, is the man who has linked himself by chains of love and culture with the wealth of the past and the promises of the future.

A few geniuses are able to achieve immortality in the creation of an unforgettable symphony, a priceless painting, an imperishable book. Most of us, however, have to be content with humbler contributions to the thought progress of the world. Our little fragments of ideas become part of the anony-mous culture of the world. Our living immortality is found more concretely in our children, in our children's children. We may not be sculptors, able to hew immortal statues out of immobile rock. Most of us, however, have the infinitely greater privilege (which we take too much for granted) of molding the spiritual life and destiny of the generations that come after us. Men and women whom we influence by the example of our lives, the children who are touched by the flame of our spirits—it is in them that we live on and find our eternal sig-nificance.

The necessity for conquering grief and adjusting to the thought of our own mortality is heightened now because we have recently passed through a time when grief and death were familiar experiences in a warring world. In many coun-tries death has become so ugly and human life so unbearable that it may prove impossible for multitudes there to retain psychic balance and sanity. All the more reason, then, for the millions of Americans living far distant from the scenes of carnage to make the achievement of moral resoluteness and courage in the presence of death a kind of ethical obligation —a determination to keep ourselves sane as the guarantors of the human future.

As a matter of fact, the real tragedy of our time is not so much that men die but that men are forced to die so pre-maturely and in many parts of the world so brutishly, without any of the enhaloing dignity of a free, peaceful, human death. The unforgivable crime of our time is that millions of men are not granted either the leisure or the opportunity for the fulfillment, even partially, of the possibilities of *this* life.

Peace of Mind

Countless poets, scholars, sages, and scientists have long before their time been plowed beneath the harrow of destruction, and their manuscripts, melodies, and formulae are forever locked in bones prematurely condemned to fertilize a seemingly unrepentant earth. It is man-made cruelty which brings death all too soon to the human race, and cuts human life off almost at the beginning of its song.

The tragedy of this untimely interruption of human existence has been expressed in a poem by the greatest modern Hebrew poet, Bialik, describing life as the harp string forever waiting to be plucked—waiting for the finger of its master that never comes. We live in a world where millions of strings shall remain unplucked. Multitudes of youths came to their sunset with many a melody unrendered. No one of us can know when the Angel of Death will come to claim him. We are subject to the Damoclean sword at any moment. Tension and disease— these stalk a universe without frontiers or barriers today. There are no customs officers who can exclude menace and danger as aliens from our lives now.

In this world of constant crisis we need the perspective that religion and psychology together can give us as we confront the mystery of death. We have learned what we must do psychologically in order to accept and to conquer grief at the loss of others. We also should know how to face the thought of our own passing, to recognize that we need not fear death or dying ourselves, but can confidently live today, trusting the universe to take care of tomorrow.

And while we live, we should try to make each day a year as far as beauty, nobility, and a warm sense of brotherhood are concerned. In a time when there is so much cruelty abroad

142

Intimations of Our Immortality

we must generate the oxygen of love to keep the soul of the world still breathing. Religion should summon all of us to deepen the quality of life as a compensation for the diminution of its quantity, to treasure each other in the recognition that we do not know how long we shall have each other, to make life strong and brave and beautiful as our answer to the forces of death abroad in the world. We must make up for the threatened brevity of life by heightening the intensity of life. The crimes and sin for which there should be little forgiveness during this epoch are hardheartedness, selfishness, mutual cruelty, lovelessness—all of the little weapons which we use to shorten the lives of others. Our very understanding of each other can serve to deepen life even when we cannot lengthen it.

All men today need the healthy-mindedness of Judaism, the natural piety with which the Jew declares, "One world at a time is enough." For just as we can rely without fear upon the Power greater than ourselves during this earthly journey; just as we can rest and do rest securely upon the bosom of mystery every time we fall asleep at night—so we can trust the universe beyond time also, recognizing that it is the part of wisdom not to seek to remove the veil from before birth or after death, but to live fully, richly, nobly, here and now, and make possible a society where other men can so live.

All over the world today there are fathers, mothers, and young wives who remember the songs of youths whose lives were brief in duration—songs of freedom defended and of humanity guarded. While we can never minimize the sadness of young melodies cut off in the first stanza, we are also quite certain that the singers of these songs, young aviators and sailors and brave young soldiers at their posts of freedom, would wish the living not to weep too long, but would remind us that there was a kind of fulfillment in their fleeting days of courageous and sacrificial living better than the futility of cowardly decades, and at the same time would challenge us to fulfill the pledges for which they have been called upon to die.

We should remember the difference between the two meanings of "end" which are found in the human language: the one *finis* and the other *telos*. Death has often written *finis* to a life that has had no "end," no "purpose." The worst tragedy that can befall a human being is to come to the end *(finis)* without ever having possessed any end *(telos)*—without ever having sought for any great aim in the midst of his life career. Those who struggled and sacrificed for freedom did possess the consciousness of an end—a purpose—in their striving, even though *finis* was their poignantly and unjustly premature fate.

We must strive in the midst of our grief to fulfill their "telos," to build a world where men will not need to perish with their mature songs still unsung, a world where human beings will need only to learn to adjust to normal grief rather than to bear abnormal sorrow and tragedy—a world that will provide all men with the opportunities for self-fulfillment—a world where the Angel of Death shall come not like a brutal robber to snatch us away before we have even greeted the noonday sun, but like a friend at eventide to lead us home after a long day when the air still is vibrating with the songs of life richly fulfilled.

CHAPTER EIGHT

Thou Hast Enthralled Me, God

"In Thy will is our peace," cries Dante in the *Paradiso,* genuflecting before the throne of God. The cry did not originate with Dante, nor did its echo die in his pages. The humble acknowledgment that all peace proceeds from God, and that to find it we must find Him, has been the sum of man's wisdom from time immemorial. In every age poets, philosophers, and mystics join with ordinary believers in the immortal chorus: "There is no rest till we find rest in Thee."

Fortunate the soul that has found its lodgment in the space-less dimensions of Divine love! More to be desired than fine rubies is the sure knowledge that we are part of Him, that His strong will contains and supports us as a mighty ocean contains and supports the infinitesimal drops of every wave. Those who possess this sense of cosmic "at-homeness" walk the highways of life with inner serenity.

But a common observation of any minister or psychiatrist today is that vast numbers of modern men and women are unable to affirm Divinity. Or, if they do believe in God, they have such a childish conception of Him that it fails to stand up in times of stress and crisis. This weak or nonexistent faith turns out to be the underlying cause of much of the contemporary feeling of depression and inner torment. As one such sufferer confided in me, "If I lose faith in an earthly friend—if a business associate fails me, if my wife proves false—there is always the possibility of finding new anchorage in another and better human being. But when I lose faith in the reality of God —as I now have—where then can I turn?"

Like many of my colleagues, I have wrestled with a number of these non-believers in the dark night of their souls, attempting to reassure them with such rational comfort as I might command. But for years I hit my head against the stone wall of their imperviousness to logic. Gradually I have come to see that all the rational arguments used on many atheists and agnostics are futile because words do not, and cannot, touch the real causes of their disbelief.

At times, it is true, the color of logic seems to tint *their* argument. They point to the frightful devastation laying waste the human landscape—atomic bombs, devouring pestilence, and withering poverty—and ask, "How can the existence of God be reconciled with this vast and overspreading evil?" This, indeed, is a realistic question, which I will deal with on a later page. But for the present I wish to suggest that such arguments are merely the reflection of the sufferer's own inner conflict, aggression and cruelty, projected upon the larger canvas of the universe.

The Denial of God's Existence

Atheism at bottom means the inability of a man to utter an all-embracing "yea" to existence. It is the denial of meaning in life. It is the distrust of the universe. The atheist's real creed might be reduced to these sentences: "I honestly believe that this world is an accidental creation of exploding suns, a place of terror and of death. I honestly believe that man is an animal who happens to be endowed with more cunning than the rest of the animal kingdom—so don't try to convince *me* that there is a superintending Deity who watches over me with love!"

This dark creed stands in absolute opposition to the outlook of religion, which, in essence, maintains that the universe is friendly, that man is trustworthy, and that God exists. Now, it may be that some men come to their anti-religious position through pure reason: I have never met one. More often the elaborate structures of atheism and pessimism, buttressed by all kinds of rational arguments, are built upon foundations of emotional conflict and disturbed human relationships in the early years of life.

The atheist himself may be unconscious of this, and will bitterly resist any psychological interpretation of his atheism. Yet this is what happened: as a child he was prepared to believe his father implicitly, to trust his mother devotedly. Then, somewhere in the crucial years of his development, in some very important area of his life, his parents let him down catastrophically. In his unconscious he condemned them as untrustworthy and faithless. From such a tragic failure in interpersonal relations early in life, the psychological leap is made to the conclusion, "The universe is untrustworthy and faithless." I believe that much atheism has the ground prepared for it in the disillusionment with the parent which has arisen in the child. Disbelief in life, skepticism about humanity, the denial of God—all sink their roots in the soil of emotion long before exposure to courses in philosophy and science. Life has scarred such people early and has made them unwilling to believe either in man or in God.

The Types of Unbelievers

Vanity sits in strange quarters, and odd, indeed, are some of the reasons men adduce for their private forms of atheism. I had a man come to me recently who proudly hung his particular brand of disbelief on the intellectual peg of Darwin and Haeckel. The struggle for existence fascinated and overwhelmed him. All life was "fang and claw," "survival of the fittest." On brief questioning, the following facts emerged. He was a younger son in a large family whose domestic fortunes had been wrecked by a cruel, domineering, shiftless father. This feckless parent was a drunkard and despot, ready with blows from either hand. In this wretched home bread was a variable, often nonexistent, entity. The bread of love, in particular, was denied this boy and his brothers, who were constantly engaged in desperate struggles for existence. (No wonder Darwin appealed to him!) Now, this particular boy, attending religious school, was taught that God's love sheltered and fed all of His creatures; even the sparrow's fall was noticed. On the child's plastic soul stuff the horrible disparity between the reality of his tyrannical father and the picture of a benevolent heavenly Father was ineradicably carved. In his young heart he learned to scoff at this "myth" of a good heavenly Father. His scoffing was later whetted to intellectual keenness by his reading of evolutionary philosophers who stressed the unrelenting struggle for survival.

This man ultimately developed into a hard, granitelike per-

Thou Hast Enthralled Me, God

sonality always trying to take vengeance upon those around him. He succeeded in accumulating a great deal of money as the result of his ruthlessness. His atheism served him well until a great emotional crisis cracked his armadillo shell. Then frightened and heartsick at the barren horizons of his life, he came to me for help. He said: "I cannot find love or *meaning* in anything, because there is no love or meaning in the universe." I was able to point out to him that all of his life he had been generalizing from one experience with a nonrepresentative father, and that he had never given himself the opportunity to see the love, the decency and human goodness in life and in the world. I showed him that his atheism was merely the shifting of a grudge onto God because of his own understandable disappointment with his human father.

Quite another type of atheism is that born of adolescent rebellion—a pattern which hardens into world attitudes of hostility. The strange thing is that persons with these beliefs are really quite tender and loving. There came to my office an attractive man of thirty-five, actively engaged in many radical causes and movements. He had thrown his splendid energies into extreme types of social reformism, but found that these pursuits were not giving him the peace of mind for which he so ardently sought. His dissatisfaction with himself and his life became so acute that in desperation he turned to me—albeit with a skeptical grimace.

"Try and do something for me" was his tacit challenge. In our very first interview the crucial facts came out. As a child he had enjoyed warm, loving relations with his father and mother, but at the onset of adolescence his own expanding virility clashed with the powers that ruled the home. Inevitable disagreements ensued, as result of which he rejected the whole structure of his parents' world, including their social and religious attitudes. And when the parental idols toppled from their pedestal, God toppled with them. Twenty years of radical opposition to existing forms of state and society had not brought satisfaction to his essentially loving nature. He was taking a vast post-adolescent detour of rebellion, and when he acquired insight into the causes of his footsore and soul-wearying struggle and flight, he had the wisdom once again to affirm life rather than negate it. The remarkable thing was that he continued with his radical interests, but now they were based on maturely conceived possibilities of a better world rather than on the angry protest against the domineering world of his parents. (He actually smiled when I pointed out to him that a radical career which had started as an endocrine upheaval had continued long past the period of glandular change.) Part of the great new world that he was now able to envision was the concept of a trustworthy and creative Divinity.

Francis Thompson, the mystic poet, has God say in *The Hound of Heaven:* "All things betray thee, who betrayest Me." This sense of forsakenness is understandable in a Christian mystic, but what shall we say to a cold-blooded scientist who, surveying his test tubes and retorts, is overcome by the empty loneliness of his laboratory? Ordinarily, such a man does not seek the advice of either the religionist or the psychiatrist. So arrogant is he in his mastery of the visible material world that he scorns the doctors of the intangible soul. However, I did happen to meet a fine specimen of this type recently at a dinner party. I saw at once by his masklike visage and sternly

Thou Hast Enthralled Me, God

disciplined manner that he was one of these test-tube realists—
and proud of it. He was condescendingly lucid in his discussion of the latest molecular research; my interest in it led to
an after-dinner conversation. While we were talking, he made
it unmistakably clear that he was an atheist. "I do not want
to hurt your feelings, Doctor," he began, "but I am quite
convinced that religion is an emotional jag, necessary perhaps
for weaklings and cowards, but unacceptable to the mind
trained in objective science."

I nodded. The type was familiar to me. Characteristically,
these men are repressed, ashamed of emotion, fearful of the
consequences to themselves if their heart valves ever open to
their fullest extent. Habitually such men turn to science for its
vaunted "controls"—and my friend was a marvelous illustration of the type. Little by little, seeing him over a period of
months in casual meetings, I discovered the underlying causes
of his emotional frigidity.

It seems that he had been brought up by an uncle (his father
having died when he was very young). This uncle was one of
those quartz-hard New Englanders who hated all emotion, a
descendant of those early Calvinists to whom all pleasure was
the invention of Beelzebub. An exact man, a precise man, a
case-hardened man, contemptuous of sentiment, but withal
very successful in the concrete realm of bills and notes. As to
God, my friend never knew whether his uncle believed in Him
or not, for any public mention of Him was in highly bad taste.

It was obvious to me that my scientist acquaintance was a
full-fledged case of hero identification with his taciturn uncle.
Tutored in rigidity from childhood, he could not break the
icy dams of restraint laid upon his emotions by his adult

model. In science he sought that perfect refuge from emotion —that bloodless realm of neutrons and protons where service to abstract truth does not involve personal commitments. In his extreme fear of such commitments he abjured God; indeed, had demolished Him entirely. It was too late—in fact, impossible—to reach the core of his iceberg nature to thaw him out. I quote his case here merely to cover the legion of similar characters whose atheism is a flight from love, a paralyzing fear of sentiment and emotion, and a reduction of life, with all of its majesty, warmth, and grandeur, to the chilled confines of a laboratory. Life has forced them to make a virtue out of their own emotional deficiencies. If they want to take pride in them they are deluding no one but themselves, incidentally losing much of the happiness that comes from man's relatedness to the universe of God.

These, then, are a trio of atheists—three portraits chosen at random from a large gallery. How astonished these brave God-deniers would be (and usually are) to discover that their cherished credo of independence springs from lovelessness in early childhood, endocrine disturbances in adolescence, or a covertly hysterical fear of emotion in adulthood! To such roots as these many cases of atheism are traceable. Nor does this psychological analysis begin to exhaust the infinite combinations of personal and social factors subtly responsible for the life-denying and God-negating creeds of modern men and women. And dynamic psychology is the modern trumpet of Joshua at whose sound the walls of many pitiful Jerichos fall —the walls of atheism and pessimism composed of the seemingly indestructible boulders of science and logic. And when the walls tumble, we see in the heart of the city not happy, mature personalities, but cowering, conflict-torn, whimpering children.

It must be admitted that there are some men and women who believe themselves to be atheists on purely intellectual grounds; self-sacrificing and creative workers in the vineyards of science are sometimes so conditioned by their "objective" and "factual" approach to everything that they regard it as insincerity on their part to use the name "God." Philosophically they are opposed to any cosmic generalization, afraid of asserting anything that is beyond the realm of demonstrable fact. They are so modest in their claim to knowledge that the very thought of God dismays them. They regard it as unjustified presumption on their part to assert Divinity—an assertion which implies some cognition of the infinite. We must understand, though we do not share, that rare type of atheism found among profoundly ethical and humanity-serving individuals which springs not from childhood frustration, adolescent disillusionment, or adult feelings of intellectual inferiority, but rather from a genuine humility about knowledge-claims and a kind of reluctance to transcend the limits of the factual.

Agnostics and Weak Believers

A subtle refinement of self-torture that goes on in the minds of many persons is the agnostic doubt with which they are constantly flogging themselves like the Penitents of the Middle Ages. In their highest reaches they are frequently gifted and intellectually alert persons constantly delving into the latest works on science and philosophy, poignantly in quest of a satisfying answer to the eternal query, "How can I believe in God?" They are like the damned spirits in Dante's *Inferno,* condemned to be whirled forever on the shifting winds of opinion and emotion. It is awfully difficult to understand sometimes why such people do not have the hardihood to reject God outright or the courage to embrace Him entirely. They are cloven souls, and the world is full of them.

Their plight is often traceable, we now know, to a wedge driven into their souls in its early formative stages—the wedge of inconsistency between deed and creed. Some homes are consistent both in action and in theology. In these homes harshness prevails in life, and vengeance is the predominant attribute of God; or again, tenderness and love rule both parental action and parental theology. The *inconsistent* home is one in which the parents are warm and loving in their action, but whose God is stern and avenging. The child in such a home will ofttimes suffer from spiritual schizophrenia—the victim of a faith that is continually vacillating between love and fear. Many agnostics and victims of cosmic instability come to this inner uncertainty because in early childhood they lived in an atmosphere of unconscious conflict between their parents' way of living and their parents' way of believing. The father acted one way and believed another. He acted with love and believed in the God of fear or, vice versa, acted with cruelty and believed theoretically in the God of love. That early environmental dualism is the seedbed of later religious uncertainty, conflict, and unhappiness.

Now, not only atheism and agnosticism but also certain forms of theism can only be understood genetically—as derivatives of childhood experience. There is a vast difference

between a sick-minded theism and a healthy-minded theism,
between morbid faith and mature faith. There is such a thing
as false piety, masquerading in all of the garments of prayer
and ritual, just as there are false love and false grief. Religion
can be grateful, indeed, to psychology for exposing childish
God ideas for what they are—illusions and emotional distortions—grateful because the elimination of infantile notions of
God will clear the ground for the growth of a truly adult idea
of God.

This psychological analysis of certain forms of atheism and
theism will appear blasphemous to many traditional religionists. They will accuse us of reducing the religious consciousness of God to some childish residue, some deposit of parental
frustration or fulfillment, in the dregs of memory. The mystic
will say, "I know God directly and my communion with Him
is both ineffable and unanalyzable. I know God as intimately
as I know the sun or my own breathing. I reject all of your
psychological dissections." The traditional religionist will say,
"I know God through my reason and through revelation. God
spoke to the human race in eternal and unchanging accents
at Mt. Sinai. He created us; He calls to us; He is the Eternal
Thou over and against my restless little 'I'. God is not a concept of the human mind. He is the transcendent reality. He is
certainly not a projection of our psychological experiences or
emotional needs. You degrade God in all of His majesty with
your analytical subtleties, and if you insist that atheism is
often to be explained away as a result of childhood *frustration*, should not belief in God likewise be explained as the
result of childhood *residues?*"

The answer in many cases is, "Alas, yes." The world is full

of people whose religious beliefs, firm though they be, are immature and stunted. In my work I come across many people who nurse inadequate notions of Divinity. Recently a woman came to me in great distress. She had lost a beloved son in the war. "Why," she cried out, "does this have to happen to me? I have always been a good woman and have tried to do the right thing. I have observed the holidays and the festivals, and now look how God has treated me. Oh, the wasted years of prayer—and now this is my reward."

I could sympathize with her all-too-human reactions in the face of such overwhelming grief, but, at the same time, I had to observe that her notion of God was immature and stunted. She was saying in effect, "If God will not suspend the great mystery of death in my special case, I withdraw my belief in Him. I will not worship Him any more." To her, God was someone to be believed in if He was good to her; denied if He did not respond to her naïve pleas.

There are many people whose God belief is highly conditional. It is an "if-then" proposition (if God is good to me, then I will believe in Him), a faith depending upon a constant flow of favors in their direction.

Again, every religious leader has countless worshipers in his congregation who subscribe to a *Green Pastures* idea of Divinity. To them the Lord is a master chef at a gigantic fish fry—a cosmic bellhop who should respond to their every summons. Many who smile at the childish credulity of the *Green Pastures* God, with all of its simple Negro symbolism, will, if they examine their own concepts honestly, find that there is very little difference between their God and Marc Connelly's picture of "De Lawd."

Thou Hast Enthralled Me, God

There are some who will say that my analysis of religious belief is just a caricature of that belief. To such I reply, "Is it not an ultimate gain, rather than a loss, to have revealed the emotional fallacies involved in a primitive, highly anthropomorphic Father dwelling in the sky? Is it not a gain rather than a loss to dissolve such an untenable God idea in the acids of psychologic analysis? After all, we human beings in the course of our experience do not discover any external heavenly replica of an earthly father sitting in the sky. Such an idea of God can lead only to a later disillusioned atheism."

My Personal Credo

In the face of these manifest and manifold diseases afflicting man's soul is there any hope for a healthy, mature religion in contemporary life? The answer is very definitely and positively, "Yes"; all nature resounds with the affirmations of God, and it remains only for man to hearken to these divine reverberations in his own soul.

One man's spiritual Odyssey may be of interest to others seeking peace of mind, because it may reflect something of the alternating turbulence and tranquillity of our modern age. I offer my experience—in no way exceptional—for whatever help it may give to my perplexed contemporaries.

To begin with, I have gone through a number of stages in my own thoughts on God. I shared in my childhood the usual picture of Divinity—a daguerreotype, as it were, of my grandfather—a heavenly replica of an old, bearded, patriarchal figure. Later, as a theological student, I lived through anguished years when nothing in the external world could stifle the question, "Where is God? What is His nature?" I realize now that my adolescent sufferings were a disguise for a deeper distrust of life, a sense of personal uncertainty. Yet I know that those adolescent years of searching for God were invaluable for my own spiritual maturation. No religious teacher who has not himself tasted of the bitter cup of rejection, agnosticism, and fear can be of help to other men and women.

During all these years there came a time when I thought that man was enough and that humanism was the answer. Traditionally, emphasis upon man and humanistic values is one of the fundamental Jewish concepts; yet I have come to see that humanism is not enough to explain man. Neither his mind nor his creative powers can be truly understood except as the offspring of some universal Parent. I have come to feel that the whole human story, with all its tragedy and its triumph, is like a page torn from the middle of a book without beginning or end—an undecipherable page when cut out of its context. The context of man is the Power greater than man. The human adventure is part of a universal sonnet—one line in a deathless poem. Without faith that our human intelligence and haunting human conscience are a reflection of a greater intelligence and a vaster creative power, the key to the cipher is lost and the episode of mankind on earth becomes a hidden code—a meaningless jumble of vowels and consonants.

The resolute atheist will, however, be unconvinced by this God-offering approach to the universe. He may admit the existence of a certain amount of order, design, and purpose in the universe, but he challenges us by saying, "You ignore the bloody and brutal disharmonies of the world; the landscape of bombed cities and blighted fields. In a world of strife, disease, and death, can you still speak of a Providential Divinity?"

For years, this query was an insoluble riddle, a menacing rock upon which my own faith dashed itself. The question was, "How can a righteous God permit so much evil and suffering in the world?" As long as I was imprisoned within the circle of traditional ideas about God, I could find no answer to this peace-destroying problem. I searched through the literature of religion and found small consolation in the famous arguments—the ontological, the cosmological, the teleological proofs for God. I read Aristotle and Augustine, Philo and Saadia, Descartes, Berkeley, Kant, and Hegel, and while I admired the towering systems which their words constructed, I found no answer for the hungry heart.

Only within recent years have I begun to discover a pathway to God that is intellectually satisfying to my own wrestling spirit. I found the first hints in the pages of Hebrew wisdom. I came to understand that the prophets in Palestine were also wrestling with the same problem. They, too, held the conviction that God was all-good, but that He did not abrogate the moral laws of life for any favorites. Those ancient prophets, in effect, said to the people of Israel, "God has established natural laws in the universe, and He expects them to operate. He has also given you consciences and minds, and He expects you to use them. If you abuse them He will not set His world topsy-turvy in order to rescue you from the consequences of your deeds."

I began to see a deep wisdom in that message—the wisdom of maturity—which does not expect God to be a Father cajoled and wheedled into violating the necessary principles of human life. I understood why Jeremiah told the people of Jerusalem (who were so confident that they were God's favorites) not to believe presumptuously that He would be partial to them and to their beloved city. There is no partiality in a moral universe. Gradually I came to understand how my ancestors were able to find the greatness of God and to discern His truth not in the eras of luxury and security, but in the catastrophe of exile, when their world was shaken to its foundations.

The unthinking man might say that during this whirlwind of national tragedy the Jews should have lost faith in God. Is there not something startling and profound in this neglected truth that the giants of the Bible found the handwriting of God not in the sunlit hours of triumph, but on the slate of tragedy? It seems like a paradox that evil and suffering should have been the birthplace of the moral God.

The very experience that now seems to make so many people atheistic is what made the prophets of Israel maturely religious. Why? Because they had gone beyond a childish view of Divinity. At a time when thousands of Jews must have been saying with their emotions, "There is no God," it was then that the prophets—Titans of the spirit—taught their new message: "God cannot do anything that will mock His moral law. He is not an Oriental monarch, to be bribed into overlooking violations of the principles upon which the earth and human society must rest."

My meditation on the prophets enabled me to make radical revision of my idea of God. At first it seems daring, if not heretical, for us to say that God is not omnipotent—that He, too, is limited. We ask in amazement, "How can God be lim-

Thou Hast Enthralled Me, God

ited? If He is not all-powerful—able to do anything that He wills—then surely He cannot be God!" I deny this conclusion. If I did not believe that God is *limited* by the very nature of the world He created, then I would have to surrender my faith.

The usual idea of omnipotence is wrong, childish, and unjust to God. There is something of the baby in every man and woman that dimly remembers a seemingly all-powerful parent. When we are very young, we think that our father and mother can achieve anything; that they are magicians who can wave a miraculous wand, transforming everything at will. Our early years give us the illusion that the parent is subject to no laws, bows to no inevitabilities. It is only as we grow mature that we discover that our human father is neither a magician nor the monarch of the world. We have to grow up to learn that God also is not a magician who changes everything in the twinkling of an eye. Maturity in our relation with our human parents means the gradual recognition of limitations and necessities to which they are subject. Maturity in the religious realm means surrendering our childish view of God and of understanding that He, too, in building a predictable world, governed by law, voluntarily surrenders something of His sovereignty.

This fact lies at the basis of much so-called "evil" in the world. Take, for example, the property of water. When God created water He endowed it with the properties of floating ships and turning millwheels. These are accounted good. But in the very nature of water is its inherent capacity to drown us.

And so it is with all other laws of nature—in their very orderliness is the guarantee that God is. That orderliness, however, limits the range of His whim and caprice.

Peace of Mind

So much for an example from the physical realm. A similarity can easily be established in the moral order. Just as God made water with its powers for good and evil, so He made man a vessel of His energy, endowed with unlimited powers of good and evil. The same force which gives man the ability to conquer adversity, to overcome disaster, can become towering white rage that commits murder. Man's highest attributes are summoned into action by this necessity of making moral choices. This very fact provides us with the answer to the die-hard atheist question, "Why did not God make man incapable of doing wrong?" If God had chosen to do this, the human race would now be a species of moral marionettes, dangling from His finger tips. Man would have been deprived of his noblest faculty: the power to choose right instead of wrong.

No, God should not be made the scapegoat for the evils that men commit. By reserving to all of us the power to work out our own destinies, God has shown His greatest wisdom. He has made us individuals when He could have made us robots, and it is this genius of individualism, this divine gift of the capacity to follow one's own moral intuition and make one's own moral decisions, which is the true hope of the world.

We believe in individuality; in the value of independent growth; in the creativity of personal responsibility. We reject the theory that men should be made good by statute, by co-ercion, by compulsion. Let us realize that this truth applies also to God's relations to man. If we really want individuality and freedom for ourselves, we dare not ask God to nullify both by making it impossible for us to commit evil. God then would become a Divine Tyrant and we would all be slaves in His dictatorship. Let us not seek to defend democracy on earth

162

Thou Hast Enthralled Me, God

and yet demand moral tyranny from Heaven. A world where human beings would possess no individuality and would have no responsible self-decisions to make would be an evil and not a good world. It may sound like a paradox, but one of the proofs of the existence of a moral God is the reality of this kind of world, where man is given the freedom to achieve destruction or salvation through his own tremendous choices.

But we do not want man to be a mere individual, isolated and alone. We want to belong together, to influence and to be influenced by our social relatedness. There is nothing more frightening than absolute aloneness. God has made an earth where we are not alone, where what we do inevitably affects an ever-widening circle. It is the glory and the tragedy of the earth that we are all involved in each other. We certainly benefit from this interlocking of our destinies. You and I as individuals did not create electric lights or sulfa drugs (an original discovery of Germany, by the way) or symphonic scores, but in this mutual world we are all recipients of the blessings that we did not create. What a price we pay for our social interdependence! The innocent suffer because the evil that men do spreads like a dark stain through the fabric of life. This is truly tragic. But the alternative would be even more so. Such an alternative would mean that we would have to be windowless little souls hermetically sealed off, not only from mutual evil, but also from mutual good. Society is God's gift to this earth, and our mutual involvement may yet be made His supreme benediction.

I do not maintain that the foregoing pages are a complete answer to the problem of evil. There is no complete answer either in atheism or in theism. I do feel, however, that this is

the more logical and rational solution. I know that there come
moments when we yearn for God to intervene dramatically in
our personal and social destinies; when we want Him to be
inconsistent with the logic of His laws and miraculously remove the pain from our hearts and the incredible cruelty from
among nations. That is a normal and natural yearning—that
yearning to have God prevent our own individual tragedy or
forestall some threatening event. However, we must discipline
ourselves to realize what we are asking; to know that it is the
cry of a child to have the father ignore or wipe away all of the
laws of human and social existence; to abolish the principles
of moral gravitation; to shield mankind from the inevitable
consequences of its own folly and weakness.

When I think with my mind rather than feel with my heart,
I cannot conceive of a world where God would interfere ca-
priciously with personal and social destiny, making all human
effort and human striving worthless. We cannot look to God
to save us from man-made evil, whether it be a civic catastrophe born out of negligence or greed or whether it be a
dictatorship that mankind long knew would slay the innocent
if it were not stopped in time. We dare not run to God to wipe
away by a miracle the effects of our human misdeeds. We cannot have only the blessings that come with mind and conscience and that distinguish us from the lifeless rock and expect God to be our heavy insurance policy against all of the
dangers and the failures of life.

God must indeed be filled with sorrow as He sees how the
human race has misused its freedom of choice and how it has
violated His moral laws. "Men, men," He could cry, "I gave
you an earth ribbed with veins of diamonds and gold and

black with frozen heat. I gave you strong and dynamic waters to drive your windmills and make your turbines hum with power. I gave you rich loam upon which you could grow waving wheat. What have you done? My coal often you have stolen, leaving only the slag for the poor. My diamonds, my gold, my living waters, you have imprisoned behind the walls of your selfish greed. Because you refused to use my gifts in order to build a just earth, you have been forced to spend gold like water for ships blown up in the twinkling of an eye. You have seen your cities ruined and your precious sons annihilated on a thousand battlefields. Now, at last, the intelligence which I have implanted in you, O race of man, has fashioned the key to unlock My treasure house of energy. Within the secret heart of my atoms is the power of life and death for all of you. O men, will you this time choose weapons of death or tools of life; unconditional destruction or unconditional survival?"

The Meaning of Revelation

What we really need today is a new conception of revelation. Traditionally, revelation took place at Mt. Sinai. God spoke to man through the Divine Book or the chosen personality of His prophets and saints. Actually, revelation should be defined as a daily concurrence with God using many human instruments as the channels of His divine message. A good friend, a loving mother, or a heroic leader is merely a vessel containing divinity in the same way that pitchblende contains the inexhaustible energy of healing radium.

To conceive of God as the power of love and creation, the

source of human fulfillment and salvation, is not projection or subjective illusion, because the universe objectively justifies such a conception of God. This is a world of relatedness, of enormous creative energy, an endless reservoir of love and truth and beauty. True, there are negative and evil factors at work in the world, but as the philosopher Whitehead has pointed out, these are neither the stable nor the victorious elements in the sweep of history. They are ultimately subordinate to the affirmative, life-sustaining potencies of existence.

God is revealed to man daily in the humble thornbushes of fine men and women. It is legitimate to move from the perspective of goodness first reflected through the character of a wise father and a good mother to the view of the universe as God's field of operation. Such a view of God rooted first in the little society of the family in its best and most loving form and then extending its horizon to the Infinite is mature and indestructible.

We cannot be said to "project" God. Rather we confront Him. The word "confrontation" really is the great word in the religion of today and tomorrow. It means coming face to face with the Divine personality which is truth-demanding, love-creating, justice-seeking in its nature.

In a sense what I am trying to say about revelation is that there are more attributes of God that we discover and confront all the time than Spinoza ever dreamed of. We confront love, sympathy, and relatedness. They are there just as the law of gravity is there. They exist as God's framework for the world. These attributes and their negatives, the obstacles to human fulfillment, are not just projected by us into the universe; they are overwhelmingly present in reality.

Thou Hast Enthralled Me, God

We human beings not only confront values; we embody them, incarnate them, channel them. We are their transmitters, spectra dancing with their light. The important thing for us to determine is what kind of ambassadors of the Divine we will become. The way we live our lives will determine whether we represent or misrepresent the country of God, whether by our cruelty we invite belief in the Demonic, not in the Divine, or by our creative compassion we truly become His accredited ministers.

It is true that we can never actually define God, since we human beings are so limited and our language is always inexact, and we shall probably always have to use metaphor and analogy in order to interpret Divine reality. What many people do not understand is that our scientific description of the universe is just as metaphorical as the religious description. Men thought that they were being very exact and scientific when they called the world a great machine. Is that not an analogy, a metaphor? Whenever we speak of reality as a machine or as purely material, we are reading something into the world. Why should we continue to interpret the universe in terms of the lowest that we know rather than in terms of the highest that we experience? Intelligence, purpose, and personality, the will to live, the need to love, the yearning to be related—these are just as important clues to reality as atoms and electrons. It sometimes seems to me that our habit of looking at the universe in terms of matter rather than in terms of purpose and of conscience is a reflection of our inferiority complex—as though we human beings were not worthy to be regarded as mirrors of the Divine. Perhaps this is part of that spiritual self-deprecation which is always fashionable in certain theological circles. There is no logical reason, however, why we should explain reality always by reducing the complex to the simple. Why exalt the atom as the clue to truth and ignore the mind of man? Why should we not believe that that which is highest in ourselves is a reflection of that which is deepest in the universe—that we are children of a Power who makes possible the growing achievement of relatedness, fulfillment, goodness?

We may not ever come to know God's essence, but His attributes of activity—namely, the universal laws of social, mental, and moral health—these we can possess. God, as Hocking insists, is not the Healing Fiction but the Healing Fact, and we come upon Him at work in the majesty of nature and the fruitfulness of mind, in the laws of atoms and the goals of men.

The maladjusted man, the neurotic woman, can worship God only morbidly. *Freedom from morbid distortion is the beginning of religious insight!* When on the basis of the human samples that we know of decency and love, we arrive at the conclusion that this is a universe on the side of decency, such an interpretation of the world is not whistling in the dark. Man does not have to read love and reason into the universe, because he already finds them there. He does not have to project these qualities into the world, since we encounter them daily in our own intimate personal experience.

Such an approach to God is dynamic, not static. It means that we come to a *reconstructed* God idea, one that is more mature and less vulnerable. Our new idea of God does not

Thou Hast Enthralled Me, God

mean that God Himself has changed, but that we have changed as we have grown in insight and experience.

There are many voices today calling for the achievement of psychological maturity in relation to God—among them, Dr. Harry Emerson Fosdick, President Julius Seelye Bixler of Colby College, the Reverend Doctor Nathan Krass and Professor Mordecai Kaplan. Professor William Ernest Hocking, in his book *Science and the Idea of God,* makes these significant comments: "God is not to be the valet for my private wishes; He is not to disrupt for human ends the order of Nature established by Him for the foundation of the world. All thoughtful religious consciousness is inclined to consider God's action in a less physical form than primitive notions assume—We should think of God as the *element* of *objectivity* in the order of values—the wide frame of meaning . . . God is the Cosmic Demand for rightness . . . The Law of normal mental life." For Professor Hocking, God is the symbol of the worthful totality which in turn confers worth and lovableness upon man. God is the trait of goodness in the universe, the goal quality in life, the presence of purpose in the nucleus of the world. Here is a mature, new interpretation of Divinity.

Another mature God idea is found in the writings of Professor Mordecai Kaplan, a great Jewish theologian, who speaks of God in very profound terms. To him the belief in God is essentially the belief in the inherent worthwhileness of life. We experience God when we realize that, despite the obstacles to man's salvation, there are enough forces in the world which can be depended upon to achieve it. Kaplan expresses his faith in the following words:

Peace of Mind

GOD THE LIFE OF NATURE

God is the Oneness
That spans the fathomless deeps of space
And the measureless eons of time,
Binding them together in act,
As we do in thought.

He is the sameness
In the elemental substance of stars and planets,
Of this our earthly abode
And of all that it holds.

He is the unity
Of all that is,
The uniformity of all that moves,
The rhythm of all things
And the nature of their interaction.

God is the mystery of life,
Enkindling inert matter
With inner drive and purpose.

He is the creative flame
That transfigures lifeless substance,
Leaping into ever higher realms of being,
Brightening into the radiant glow of feeling,
Till it turns into the white fire of thought.

God is in the faith
By which we overcome
The fear of loneliness, of helplessness,
Of failure and of death.

170

Thou Hast Enthralled Me, God

God is in the hope
Which, like a shaft of light
Cleaves the dark abysms
Of sin, of suffering, and of despair.

God is in the love
Which creates, protects, forgives.
His is the spirit
Which broods upon the chaos men have wrought
Disturbing its static wrongs,
And stirring into life
The formless beginnings
Of the new and better world.

l believe that God is the Power for salvation revealing Himself in nature and in human nature, in networks of relationships, in countless situations and fields of operation where evil is vanquished and goodness triumphs. God is in the pain of growth, in the seed of sorrow, in the lure of thought, and in all the laws of fulfillment which bind men and stars together.

A New God Idea for America

To come to a new idea of God will require genuine growth and maturity on our part. It may well be that in this age, when we realize we must give up our old ideas about economics, isolationism, and national sovereignty, we shall also come to a new idea of God—an idea that will reflect America's democratic experience and culture. The best scientific and philosophic minds of our century—men like Whitehead and Compton—agree that we need to look upon God as the Power who needs our collaboration, and who looks to man to be His mature partner in the developing evolution of a better world.

That notion was contained in our Jewish tradition; but it could never be deeply felt so long as men lived in cultures that were not free and equal. How could human beings emotionally feel themselves partners of God when their daily lives showed that they were only serfs and slaves to other men? I am making the prophecy that it will be from the *democratic experience of our century that mankind will first learn its true dignity as independent and necessary partners of God.*

The story of the human race, until the age of technological democracy, has really been the story of dependence and helplessness—of men really feeling impotent in the presence of poverty and disease, of tyranny and autocracy, before which they had to bow their heads in resignation. Men may have said with their lips that God needed them as His co-workers, but they did not feel this truth with their hearts as long as life itself showed that they were not even needed as co-workers by men. The Italian peasant of the fifteenth century, for example, whose ancestors for generations had tilled the same soil, been baptized in the same church, struggled with poverty and disease in the same ignorance, depended for survival upon the good will of his feudal overlord—that peasant could not have had the idea of God that a free American can create out of his new culture.

I say that the time is coming when we have to bring our idea of God into harmony with the new realities of our life. America is different from Europe. In Europe the emphasis was too often upon obedience and dependence upon some strong power to whose will man had to submit. In America, as

Thou Hast Enthralled Me, God

the anthropologist Mead points out, the emphasis has been upon self-reliance, upon every new generation doing better than its fathers, on becoming more successful in human attainments. One of the great troubles is that in our religion we have continued to picture our relationships to God in terms of the helpless, poverty-stricken, powerless motifs in European culture. Now, a religion that will emphasize man's nothingness and God's omnipotence; that calls upon us to deny our own powers and to glorify His—that religion may have fitted the needs of many Europeans, but it will not satisfy the growing self-confident character of America.

One reason why America has not been deeply religious may very well be that we have tried to keep an idea of God that was out of tune with our contemporary life. We Americans have had little of the feeling of helplessness and of dependence that characterized so much of Oriental and European religion. We have had a continent to conquer and new social dreams to make come true. America has had the feeling that there is no limit to its conquest of nature. A civilization that has little of the father complex in it; that has ever made a virtue out of individual initiative and outstripping the father in achievement—that culture will find it increasingly difficult to submit to the idea of a dominant Father.

There is a chance here in America for the creation of a new idea of God; a God reflected in the brave creations of self-reliant social pioneers; a religion based not upon surrender or submission, but on a new birth of confidence in life and in the God of life. We can really begin to think of ourselves as *responsible co-workers with God*. In our prayers and in our religious teachings we shall have to catch up spiritually with the realities of daily living. We must be brave enough to declare that every culture must create its own God idea rather than rely upon outworn tradition. Europe and Asia too often emphasized dependence; America must emphasize independence and interdependence. It should come to its God idea not through a feeling of helplessness, but through a feeling of confidence. It will find its God not in defeat, but in social victory. It will seek Divinity not primarily through mystical surrender, but through practical moral activity. The religion of the future, for the first time, may become a partnership religion in which men will not only *say,* but will *feel,* that they are indispensable to God.

The psychologically mature God idea for our age must end the spiritual and cultural lag which separates our daily experiences from our theological formulas. God is portrayed too frequently in feudal or at least monarchical terms. In the democratic society that must be built in this postwar era, a feudal deity is out of place. The church and the synagogue alike can, if they will, help men everywhere to resist the economic and political slavery threatening to engulf human dignity and freedom, by teaching belief in a God who wants co-operation, not submission; partnership, not surrender. God, according to Judaism, always wanted His children to become His creative partners, but it is only in this age, when democracy has at least a chance of triumphing around the globe, that we human beings can grow truly aware of His eternal yearning for our collaboration.

We will become psychologically mature in our idea of God only as we come to recognize that we human beings should never expect final knowledge about Divinity. Our minds are

Thou Hast Enthralled Me, God

fragmentary beams of light, like the flashes of glowworms in a summer's night. The fleeting illumination they provide enables us to see in the midst of the darkness many wonderful summits of social achievement still attainable by the restless feet of this youthful race of men. Divinity is here both on the earth that provides the possibility of life, order, intelligence, and also in the insatiable moral hunger of man; man never quite ready to accept tyranny as natural, defeat as inevitable, society as irremediable. Religion can help us to retain the faith that, in the cosmic night, that Great Western Star, God, and the lesser stars, men, will not be extinguished to all eternity.

CHAPTER NINE

Where Religion and Psychology Part–and Meet

T HE faith-hungry heart, beating plaintively in a world of confused struggle and flight, no longer asks, "What shall a man believe?" So enormous and critical is the problem that mere intellect has been transcended; we seek not a credo or a doctrine, but a *reality* that will sustain us in the battle. We wish to discover, if possible, a core of *being* around which we may integrate ourselves, an armature on which we can wind the immortally charged threads of personality and character.

This inward core—if it is to support our soul, nerves, mind, and body—must be an alloy containing all possible and potential elements of strength. To accept a weak or spurious metal is to visit upon ourselves some of the pain, failure— even some of the catastrophe—that surround us. But if, somehow, we can fuse into the core of our being all the serene and glorious strengths now available to man, it is highly probable that inward peace of an incorruptible and more-than-human purity will be our portion in life.

The elements of this incorruptible fusion lie serviceably at hand in the revealed and joint truths of religion and psychiatry. How nobly these truths augment and buttress each other! Both are deeply concerned with the underlying realities of life. We have seen how shrewdly psychiatry documents religion and how, in turn, religion elevates and universalizes the findings of psychiatry. To those most familiar with these mutually complementary aspects of reality, it would seem that religion and psychiatry were twin angels, bending in unison to lift up ailing, bewildered man.

Unfortunately, however, there exist a number of persons —imperfectly or partially instructed—who either quail or balk at the idea that religion and psychiatry can ever agree on the terms of man's salvation. Religionists are apt to be suspicious of psychiatry, and psychiatry, on its part, has often been intolerant or contemptuous of religion. There are some religious figures who are quite determined and unyielding in their opposition to the advances of psychiatry. At times they seem to take the attitude that the attempt to relate religion to other disciplines of human truth might sully religion's purity and expose the thought of God to the profane hands of the workaday world. Such interpreters of the spirit actually compartmentalize life and divide rather than unify the human soul.

The prophets of Israel could never have conceived of religion in such narrow and exclusive terms. God for them was infinite concern for the good life, and all human and social fulfillment within that life. Great philosophers in the Jewish tradition, not to mention those in other religious traditions, welcomed rather than feared the helpful insights of science and metaphysics. Philo took much from Plato; Maimonides and Aaron ben Elijah were greatly indebted to Aristotle. All of Western religion has benefited from the cosmic discoveries of Galileo and Newton, as well as from the biological discoveries of Darwin and Huxley. Theology, which first attacked scientists as though they were callous vandals, destroying the sanctuary of God, has lived to see in the work of science a manifestation of God's activity, and to regard many scientists as reverent workmen, engaged in a consecrated quest for deeper truths about the Holy of Holies.

On this question perhaps we cannot escape temperamental differences. Some men constitutionally want religion to be confined to mystic experience with "The Wholly Other." But others of us, who look upon God as the source of salvation, would regard religion as inadequate and intolerably circumscribed unless it concerned itself with the foreground of life—namely, man, with his moral and social duties. To us, communion with God is not merely a private absorption in the eternal Thou; rather it bids us to return to the workaday world and sanctify it by all the means in our power. Such sanctification necessarily involves the use of all means that fumbling humanity has discovered in its long journey—the instruments of physical and social science, the sharp-edged sword of philosophy—and now, the healing instruments of psychology.

There is a fear in the heart of many religionists that these scientific techniques might overshadow religion and even absorb its historic functions. Again and again, the world has witnessed the shrinkage of religion's domains, owing to the expansion of science. For example, men once turned in prayer to God for rain. Now they turn to the Department of Agriculture for irrigation. Men once turned to God for escape from

Religion and Psychology

poverty; our age relies upon technology and industry and economic manipulation to bring abundance. Understandable, then, is the fear that psychotherapy, with its cure of souls, will further contract the sphere of religious influence, that religion will remain only as a fossil in an age that has turned to Marx and Freud and Einstein for salvation.

The approach of many religionists to dynamic psychology is really filled with both fear *and* misunderstanding. There is suspicion, for example, that psychology will analyze away all our human ideals and moral values, will reduce them all to some childish complex or to some infantile phobia. The truth is, however, that psychology will remove only the *infantile* aspects of our fears, frustrations, and hatreds—leaving all that is strong and mature in us as the foundation for future building.

It is undeniable that some of the great pioneers of psychiatry were antagonistic to religion. Freud's negative approach to religion was partly a reflection of his detached scientific temperament, partly a mirror of the excessive rationalism of the century in which he lived, and partly also the result of his own bitter personal experience with organized religion's intolerance of his pioneering investigations. Freud and some of his disciples have been biased, but that spiritual bias is merely an accident of their personal biographies and does not in any way invalidate the spiritual helpfulness of their discoveries about human nature. As a matter of fact, many of Freud's most reverent disciples today disagree with certain of his negative philosophical and metaphysical conclusions. It is becoming clearer that one cannot condemn all of religion because of a minority of fanatics and zealots, any more

Peace of Mind

than one can condemn all of psychiatry because of the minority of charlatans who practice in its name. When we speak of psychiatry, we should refer to its most representative and most gifted practitioners and its well-tested truths rather than its occasional aberrations, extreme hypotheses, and speculations. Likewise, religion must be viewed in terms of its saints and sages, and its profound and well-tested moral and spiritual laws and practices, rather than its tragic aberrations, intolerances, and bigotries.

Under no circumstances, however, is the fear justified that psychiatry can ever take the place of religion or render the spiritual realm obsolete. While the insights of psychiatry can be helpful to all people, psychiatry necessarily concerns itself with the abnormal, the neurotic; its main purpose is to achieve therapeutic results with maladjusted people. Religion, on the other hand, deals with men and women of all degrees of adjustment. One of its primary purposes is to bring integration and happiness to normal human beings, to give them the courage, the strength, and the serenity necessary for the good life—a purpose neither conflicting with, nor threatened by, the aims of psychiatry. Psychology must not be viewed as a competitor of religion, any more than the science of optics should be regarded as a competitor of normal vision.

The fear that psychology will take the place of religion is baseless; although the twain meet at many points, they differ profoundly both in goal and in substance. It must be understood that psychology and psychotherapy are scientific disciplines not basically concerned with moral judgments, whereas religion inevitably lives in the realm of ethical concepts. Psychotherapy is committed to utter neutrality in moral affairs and goes beyond its province when it makes "value judgments" about the total meaning of life. Religion, on the other hand, fails in its spiritual duty when it does not give men and women a perspective about their place in God's plan.

Psychiatry, as Professor Hocking points out, seeks to eliminate human misery and emotional distortion. It has the advantages of objectivity and rationality in its treatment. It ofttimes can dissolve excessive guilt feelings and destructive self-disapproval. It teaches that there is such a thing as "destructive secrecy—that inability to let oneself go, which becomes then a preying inward fire." But with all its magnificent successes, psychiatry has no authority to speak about the eternal anxieties of men concerning the nature of God and the trustworthiness of the universe. It takes religion and religion alone to assure men that "the world has a character which justifies hope and serenity."

And, finally, religion must paint the larger canvas of universal and eternal meaning. Psychiatry necessarily deals with the finite, the limited, the partial aspects of existence. Religion alone can give men awareness of the Infinite and the sense of the total significance of life—a precious relatedness to the wider frame of purpose and perfection.

Yet, while religion asserts its proper place in the aspirational life of men, rightly refusing to surrender its throne of morality and of purpose, it must likewise be willing to accept with gratitude whatever help the techniques of the laboratory can provide in the attainment of the good life.

The fact that the sanctuary has its unique contribution to make to the world does not mean that it should refuse the helpful hand of a great ally — the psychological clinic.

Peace of Mind

Rather should it rejoice in the assistance which psychological understanding can give to every divided soul. When that soul is integrated and healed it becomes released for the first time to participate in creative religious experience free from morbidity.

We must always keep in mind the limitations of dynamic psychology. It can help to liberate men from shadow fears, but it can never transform them into angels. It certainly does not guarantee to make them happy—but only less unhappy than they presently are. Psychology understands quite well that a degree of unhappiness and discontent and conflict is inevitable to our finite species. It seeks to reduce the amount of this unhappiness, at the same time realizing that certain difficulties must remain as long as man is what he is. It knows that it can only prepare the ground for the good life, but cannot of itself guarantee goodness. Such a guarantee can be provided only by religion and its compelling goals.

Nor is dynamic psychology a panacea for human ills. It ignores ofttimes the social sources of human misery, the wars and poverty of men. It is no cure-all (it never claimed to be one), but its insights will be as valuable for the religion of tomorrow as the cosmological and biological insights of the past several centuries have proved indispensable for the mature religion of today.

No, dynamic psychology will never take the place of religion, any more than biology or physics has taken the place of religion. But its insights can give to modern religion a new wisdom about the laws of individual and social health. The discoveries of the psychiatrist's clinic in the field of interpersonal relationships should inspire religion to stress new

Religion and Psychology

principles of human action, to sanction new approaches to the self, to society, and to the universe.

In order to achieve the good life, men need to believe in themselves and in human nature generally, to accept as normal the pluralism of their moods and capacities, to understand in a new sense the danger of pride, to possess some ideal human personalities with whom they can identify themselves, and to realize that emotion as well as reason is indispensable in the attainment of inner serenity and social salvation. On every one of these points—the nature of man, the sin of pride, the proper role of the hero in character development, the legitimacy of feeling—religion can gain some valuable aid from the best psychological clinics of our time and can use its influence with human beings to teach millions of normal men and women fundamental new truths about their psychic and moral needs and duties.

Some Truths That Psychiatry Adds to Religion

One is struck by the ironic fact that while Western religion spends a vast amount of time and energy condemning man as a hopeless sinner—a fouled and blackened vessel unworthy to contain the Divine ichor—psychiatry is quite optimistic, even cheerful, about human possibilities. How can this be? Psychology, which knows all about man's frailties—his overweening drives toward incest, murder, his desperate ugliness revealed in the intimate revelations of the analytic chamber—how can psychiatry be such a champion of man's better self? And this at a time when the most influential voices in theology have practically consigned man to the pit of his own

Peace of Mind

digging—a pit from which only the unmerited mercy of God can save him.

Miracle though it be, it is true that psychiatry does insist on man's essential goodness and decency. It was with real joy recently that I heard a brilliant psychiatrist friend of mine expound her views on human nature. "I believe in human beings," she said. "The more I analyze them, the more I come to see what fine creatures they potentially are." Assuming for a moment the role of devil's advocate, I determined to press her on the subject. "Our madhouses choked with insane persons, our slums teeming with delinquents, our clogged divorce-court dockets—just to mention a few symptoms that come to mind—how do you explain these?" I asked.

With a gentleness that I have seldom seen in either a clergyman or a doctor, she replied, "The unpleasant things in life make so much noise that we forget the silent operation of the good. Evil is aggressive, rampant, but good is quiet, undemonstrative. Like the law of gravity itself it is constant, irresistible, *still*. Deafened by the roaring tempests of hatred, we are apt to forget the quietly rising tide of devotion, loyalty, and compassion which brings the argosies of man safely to harbor." Two of her renowned psychiatric colleagues present at this discussion concurred in this hope-filled approach to man. It might be well if some of my clerical colleagues would stop stressing the morbid aspects of life and take a page from this analyst's notebook.

Special pleading to one side, it is undeniable that modern man is ill. His illness racks him, fills him with apprehension, acute pain. Sometimes it is a question of whether or not he will recover. Certainly he will not get well if his belief in him-

Religion and Psychology

self is constantly poisoned by a religious message which stresses his evil proclivities. It is essential that theology don the more tolerant robes of psychiatric wisdom if it is to be a true minister to our civilization and its discontents.

A concrete example will illustrate. Contrast the ineffectual homily that a minister usually serves up to a group of delinquent boys with the shrewd therapy offered by Dr. Fritz Redl in Detroit. This pioneer psychologist, working with a group of hardened youngsters from the least-privileged sections of the city, has achieved a miracle. And how? Merely by holding up before each individual boy a bright, unwavering belief in the lad's essential goodness, both as a person and as a member of society. There are plenty of things that Redl does not like about his "gang children." He tells them so. For instance, to a boy who had stolen an automobile tire, Dr. Redl said, "We do not like what you have done today, Jimmy, but we like you." The doctor knew that Jimmy had stolen the tire in order to compensate for some inward insecurity, and it was the physician's aim here to remove the cause of that insecurity by buttressing the boy's self-esteem.

This is the kernel of the psychiatric method, and there is scarcely a minister in America who could not profit by this golden technique. The same healing effect of the assurance that human nature is potentially both decent and brave was demonstrated by Colonel Grinker and Major Spiegel in their work with men under combat. Their book, *Men Under Stress,* again and again proves how vital to morale was the psychiatrist's confidence in human nature. Whether in battle or in peacetime living, it is the contagious belief in the goodness and courage of man that becomes his shield and buckler. No

Peace of Mind

one tells a man going into battle, "You are a miserable sinner, unworthy of redemption." Why, then, should this morbid approach of so much of Western religion be continued in
use during the equally shearing stresses of civilian life? Religion today could well reaffirm that faith first enunciated in
Genesis, and continually stressed in classic Judaism, that man
is truly created in God's own likeness.

Another new truth about man that religion must emphasize
now is the truth of pluralism. Man is not a single self. He car-
ries within him many selves—a happy self, a frightened self, an
angry self. Man is like an omnibus with many little egos jos-
tling each other as the vehicle of life hurtles down the highway. The great Jewish philosopher Saadia a thousand years
ago pointed out this truth about our inner pluralism. In the
last chapter of his famous work, *Beliefs and Doctrines,* he dis-
cusses the good life. He begins by pointing out that variety
and plurality are the very essence of nature and that man also
is a composite of many organs and many instincts. If we wish
to achieve the good life we shall have to arrange for a democracy among our desires and interests rather than a tyranny of
one over the others. There is a place for love, for food, for
material security, for the achievement of wisdom in the happy
life. He takes two vivid illustrations to prove his point of the
need of pluralism in human experience. He says that a single
color like yellow or blue is hard on the eyes and monotonous
on the soul. Only mixed colors, blended together, produce the
beauty of a painting. A single tone has only one effect and
becomes discord and shrillness in our ears. It is only the min-
gling of different musical notes that can produce harmony and
melody. If in the world of sight and sound, diversity is neces-

sary, how much more in the achievement of the good life must there be a co-operative democracy of our instincts and our desires.

That old philosopher can teach us today the necessity of accepting ourselves as complex rather than as simple personalities. Every man is a little country with hills and valleys, summits and depressions. Man is not just one flat plain. The terrain of the human spirit is extremely variegated. Religion must encourage us to realize that we must anticipate many deserts as well as some oases in the terrain of our soul.

The understanding that life is inescapably pluralistic does not mean that we should permit ourselves to become a disorganized chaos, a wild landscape without any organizing principle at work. Every man has the task of arranging his life into a pattern of unity, but that unity will always be a unity of diverse parts, a harmony of many varied elements. Religion should emphasize what Plato and Aristotle taught millenniums ago—that inner justice is always the creation of proportion and harmony, that the good life is the attainment of the golden mean between extremes of fear, anger, aggression, and love. Successful individual living is dependent upon the expression of the proper quantity of these qualities.

Excessive preoccupation with one drive or impulse of our nature is the enemy of inner peace. We must anticipate the presence of many qualities—negative as well as positive—in our individual make-up. As long as no single element becomes excessive in quantity we can rest assured that all of them together constitute the ingredients of creative living. By discerning the line of demarcation between too much and too little, excess and deficiency, we can fashion for ourselves a life pattern in which our pluralistic emotions will play their role—the negative ones of fear and hate being subordinated to the affirmative emotions of courage and love.

Religion, in teaching man to accept the truth of pluralism and of proportion in his inner life, can aid him to avoid rigid extremism. It can teach man that there is a time to be proud and a time to be humble, a time to be independent and a time to be dependent, a time for detachment and a time for attachment. Both Christian and Jewish ethics focus attention on the sin of pride. Rabbinic Judaism points out that uncontrolled anger and rigid pride are among the great dangers that every man faces in his emotional life. The rabbis said that "a man who becomes a slave to anger sets up a strange god in himself which he worships." They also said that "every man who is filled with an arrogant spirit is as though he had worshiped idols and denied the basic principles of religion."

Now, there is a legitimate pride in the world which reveals itself in the courageous initiative and self-reliant individualism of man the worker, the artisan, the creator. There is, however, an illegitimate pride which reveals itself in the stoical ideal of absolute self-sufficiency. Stoicism in its many forms has conspired to make men and women ashamed of their natural emotions and their transitory weaknesses. It began as a great ethical system, but its end results in many human lives have been warping and distorting. The stoical ideal in Western culture sought to make men strong. Too often it has merely made men hard. Its goal has been to toughen the fiber of human nature against the blows and defeats of fortune. But, actually, stoicism often causes men to be isolated, arrogant, making a god of self-reliance, fleeing from warm human relationships as though they were sins of weakness and of dependence.

Enlightened religion should condemn the extreme stoic way of life, since it inevitably leads to emotional callousness and to false pride. A man who tries to live life with the boastful assertion, "I always keep my problems to myself. I refuse to seek help from others because that is a confession of dependence and cowardice"—such a man has set up his self-reliant little ego as his god; he worships at the shrine of his own competence. He is a "self-made man"—and as Ring Lardner remarked: "Whenever I see a self-made man I realize how bad a job he has done."

Certainly it is true that we need to maintain independence in certain areas of life. We must not be passive but active agents in this strenuous, challenging world. At the same time, we must not make a fetish out of our self-sufficiency. It is normal and wise for us to rely at moments upon the insights, the courage, and the consolation which our human brothers can give us, knowing full well that they in turn will rely upon our gifts and strength on other critical occasions. Let us not be too proud to admit weakness at moments and to absorb strength from others in our day of need. The ruthless repression of our common human problems and fears can only make us either hard or ill; the sharing of these problems with our human comrades alone can save us from the sin of pride, the idolatry of self-sufficiency.

The latest findings of psychology emphasize the normality of "human symbiosis," which simply means, in lay language, the intertwining of our lives with those around us. This happily revises the early Freudian notion that we are weak and immature when we fail to stand, in stoic detachment, on our own two feet.

The distinguished American philosopher, Charles Morris, has described the necessity of having "proper detachments and proper attachments." By detachment I do not mean total flight from life, but rather the achievement of wise perspective —what Spinoza called "looking at things under the aspect of eternity." Detachment gives us the understanding that we are born into a world that is larger and more important than we; that we are drops in an infinite sea; that we are marvelously distilled globules of Divine rain and dew; that we shall not last forever; that all of our priceless values are at the mercy of time, and that we cannot have both intensity of experience and permanency of duration.

By detachment I mean the ability to look at ourselves with a kind of laughing humor, a nodding acquaintance with our fragilities, a tipping of the hat, as it were, to the petulant angers which vanish as we recognize them. By detachment I mean also the daring to view our individual life in the greater setting of time and eternity; to taste beforehand with the tongue of imagination the defeats and the pains to which life commits us, and by so tasting to remove something of the gall and vitriol from the cup of defeat. Man has this gift of discounting both his own victories and his own calamities. Let us utilize it to the full, for our greater peace of mind.

Not only in our personal lives, but also in the life of humanity must we have the ability to live in long-term instead of short-term values. We should know that civilization is a tougher plant than we usually imagine. Its roots are widely spread over the earth, and even when war comes as a blight

Religion and Psychology

to wither some of its tendrils, nevertheless it sends forth bud and blossom and rich fruit in other climates and at other times. We who have lived through an age of fire and hail are often too numbed to feel the coming of new life beneath our feet, or to see the promise of a new day concealed beyond the blood-red horizon. Life will not perish with us; humanity will not die when we die. Culture will not disappear with our generation or our century. We can live only with the resolve to make our best contribution to whatever culture shall survive, and to live for the triumph of men whom we shall never know, of ages that we shall never experience.

This is also maturity—spiritual maturity. Even as we are the heirs of martyrs, saints, and heroes who lived and died for us, and in their death gave birth to our conflicting world, so are we the ancestors of an unpredictable, creative, aspiring human society yet in the bourne of time.

Give Us Heroes

Contemporary psychological experiment reveals that man cannot have true inner security or fulfillment without possessing an ideal to imitate, a hero to follow. Human beings can get along without many of the physical conveniences of life much more readily than they can dispense with the experience of ideal companionship and comradeship. Concentration camps showed how men broke when they were not allowed to belong to one another or to follow some courageous martyr among them. On the other hand, men were incredibly courageous and resistant, even though deprived of material things, when they had some ideal person or pattern to keep before their eyes. Read Anna Freud's book *War and Children* and see how the youngest blitz victims maintained their morale in the midst of rubble and wreckage when they had some living and guiding hand to which to cling.

Matter—the most important thing in the world? No! Ideals! Companionship of inspiring heroes, martyrs, saints, teachers, leaders. These are the indispensables for human achievement. Man cannot live without the support of other human personalities—wise, friendly, and compassionate. We all know that the child cannot grow without reliance upon the strong adult. What is not recognized sufficiently as yet is that adults seldom outgrow that need for the ideal hero-friend. We go throughout life in continual search of men whom we can trust. We can never be cured of the yearning for higher stand- ards and codes of conduct embodied in both saints and friends.

Man loses his sense of direction when the compass of his soul is not magnetized by some great human star within the orbit of his experience. This truth has been intuitively under- stood in the realms of literature and of religion. The ancient Greeks were educated on the principle of identification with Hellenic heroes. As Professor Jaeger, in his classic work, *Paideia: The Ideals of Greek Culture,* puts it, "The most ef- fective guidance in personal difficulty is given by the lives of model heroes of old . . . the role of *example* in education. . . ." Plutarch's interest was chiefly centered upon his educational power of great examples. His biographies of great men have inspired a dozen cultures, a hundred generations. Since Homer, the very foundation of aristocratic education has been the glorification of great heroes long dead.

Religion and Psychology

Not only Hellenism, but also Hebraism was always aware of the role of the hero in the formation of character. The Jewish religion constantly stressed the virtues of the patriarchs, rehearsing the moral qualities of Moses, the lawgiver, and his immortal successors. One might even say that the educational process of Judaism depended largely upon vividly presenting to the growing minds of each new generation the deeds and the qualities of great human personalities which might serve as models for imitation. Christianity, likewise, has always recognized the influence of the ideal life of Jesus and the saints upon the mind fabric of the worshipers.

Religion has made a principle of the *imitatio dei*—"the imitation of God." But there is also a process continually going on in human life of *imitatio hominis*—"the imitation of man." The true extent of this identification process was not appreciated, perhaps, until our own age, because only now do we realize that that is not only a conscious but an unconscious process. It is tragic that so many men and women yearning for a hero find it difficult to attach themselves to any ideal personality because early in life they were captured as prisoners by some ignoble or warping leader in the little battalion of the family.

Too many people unconsciously go throughout life as camp followers of an unhappy father or a neurotic mother, fearful, insecure, shame-ridden, because in their life career they unwittingly became imitators of an unhealthy personality. Religion now has a new task presented to it by this psychological discovery of the true nature of the identification process. Religion should determine to liberate man not only from slavery to wrong ideals, but from inner slavery to unhealthy personalities, whether father, mother, older brother, or sister. Religion should encourage men and women to desert the ranks of the emotionally shackled and to enlist as volunteers in the regiment of the mature, whose commanders are the noble and the immortal heroes of the human race. For since we know that man is compelled to imitate, the only question is whether our inevitable mimicry shall involve us in enslavement to parental models often narrow, imperfect, and erroneous or whether the identification process shall occur on the higher levels. Given the choice, should we not assimilate the patterns of model heroes and heroines whose courage and nobility will provide us with a design for living that we can make our own? Religion will serve humanity best in one area of existence when it emancipates men from false, distorting, and unworthy identifications, and at the same time inspires men on both the conscious and the unconscious levels, to attach themselves to genuine heroes of the spirit.

Out of this hero-worshiping instinct in all of us, a sobering truth emerges. If we are influenced by powerful personalities around us, may not we, in turn, influence others? Yes, for better or worse, we do. Constantly, without our knowing it, we are sources of infection for good or evil. We are the carriers of health and disease—either the divine health of courage and nobility or the demonic diseases of hate and anxiety. No one can be immunized against us; as long as we live we make the world freer or more enslaved, nobler or more degraded.

This is a new and extremely sobering task, which places unsuspected ethical burdens upon each of us. Our emotions and our moods, as well as our words and our deeds, penetrate human life and make those who come in contact with us either

Religion and Psychology

the beneficiaries or the victims of our presence on earth. Depth-psychology has opened up a new dimension of ethical responsibility by showing us that what we are today helps determine the shape of tomorrow, and that our personalities will be either a blessing or a curse upon the coming generation that cannot help imitating us.

Dare Recognize Your Emotion

Sink your drill into that thinking, planning, rational-minded creature, man—the human animal of which we are so justly proud—and find an artesian well of emotion, gushing with terrific pressure from the deepest places of the soul. Psychiatry has tapped this well, named and recognized it, freed the rich fountain for creative, happy, human uses. And wisely so. For the terrifying truth about emotion is this: unless it flows and gushes freely, it will choke the soul that produces it. Yes, your soul as well as mine—because there never existed a soul that did not yearn to overflow with natural emotion.

Religion, guided by psychology, must now recognize how profoundly it has gone astray in its attitude toward emotion. Modern liberal religion has shared the mood of the last several centuries—the mood of rationalism. Perhaps this approach is comprehensible as a reaction to the excessive emotionalism of the Orthodox Church. Liberals saw how many traditional faiths wallowed in oceans of feeling, and allowed superstition and myth to govern men's destinies. Revolting against this undisciplined emotionalism, they went to the other extreme and built chilly meetinghouses upon the cold pillars of abstract reason. Modern religion, in a sense, swings between these two extremes of superstitious emotion, on the one hand, and rationalistic faith, on the other.

Now, the fear of emotion which characterizes liberal religion is part of the world mood in this epoch of history. Since the seventeenth century, men have been either afraid or contemptuous of emotion and have worshiped at the shrine of abstract reason. Feelings and qualities, as Whitehead and Mumford continually emphasize, were relegated to the realm of subjective prejudice. Reality was defined in terms of atoms and molecules, electrons and mathematical formulae. There was something terribly wrong about this deflation of human emotion, but as long as pure reason paid dividends in terms of new mechanical power and industrial victory, few noticed how lopsided life was becoming. Everybody was under the spell of impersonal science, and impersonal science sneered at feeling and despised emotion. Objectivity became the watchword of progress, and men began to be ashamed of intruding their subjective emotions into the realm of human judgment.

No wonder life began to be more shallow and humanity began to be more callous and insensitive! How could it be otherwise? Man became half human while worshiping at the shrine of pure reason; the result was that the emotions were captured by perverts and tyrants. The dictators of our age, recognizing that human beings become moral and spiritual invalids on a diet of abstract science, invaded the sphere of the emotions with their death dances and blood symbols. How close they came to capturing the globe by their cold and calculating manipulation of the emotional realm, which had been spurned and neglected by both science and religion!

We should not have been surprised at the appeal and power

of these brutal leaders. They fed the hungry spirit of man with poisonous food, but with *food*—the food of emotion! They recognized that humanity was being starved by the abstract and mechanical disciplines of physical science; that men were being treated as automata with "slot-machine minds" rather than as creative and organic personalities, nourished by emotion.

The truth should be obvious now that when no legitimate outlet is provided for the emotions of men, they will seek illegitimate outlets; that when moral religion starves the feelings of its worshipers, immoral religions like racialism and tribalism will claim its fanatics.

Liberal religion must plead guilty to a fear and contempt of emotion. The historic reasons for that fear and contempt are understandable, but a new approach is required if human life is to become whole and free again. Dynamic psychology, pioneered by Freud, can make an enormous contribution to religion in this field. Before Freud, men might justifiably look upon emotion as the primitive and childish aspect of human nature. But since Freud, it is quite clear that emotion is a major part of human life, the mother of reason, the source of art, science, literature, and religion.

Men may escape emotion with their lips, but cannot escape it with their deeds. It is the dynamic energy which vitalizes every aspect of culture, every creation of civilization. Emotion is not something shameful, subordinate, second rate; it is a supremely valid phase of humanity at its noblest and most mature.

True, emotion must not be allowed to run wild. It must be channeled and disciplined, but it should no longer be regarded as a poor relation, a slavey in the kitchen of life. Emotion, whether we recognize it or not, is the prince—often incognito, but still the prince. Let liberal religion come to recognize this truth, harness this powerful aspect of humanity to the chariot of reason, and a new era of freedom and happiness will come to the earth.

The older forms of the Jewish religion intuitively understood the part played by emotion in the collective life of Israel. The builders of Judaism utilized emotion in order to sublimate the passions, the angers, the dreams of the people. Let us look for a moment at the great holydays and festivals of Judaism; how artistically they arranged for the expression of feeling and the harnessing of emotion. The New Year and the Day of Atonement were occasions for the collective expression of sin and guilt; the participation of the entire group in this verbalization did bring cleansing and inner peace. Jews expressed, rather than repressed, their shortcomings and inadequacies and sins. Succos, celebrating the harvest season, was a great festival of rejoicing, the collective expression of gratitude accompanied by the dance and group ecstasy. Chanukkah and Purim enabled the people to express their aggressive emotions, to sublimate their feelings of wrath and hatred, and through this verbal release to achieve new serenity. Passover represented the passion for freedom, and Shevuoth the joy and the acceptance of the Law. The whole calendar of the Jewish year wisely arranged for systematic and collective-feeling outlets, the purge of the emotions, the control of the inner life by what the psychologist today would call a process of verbalization and sublimation.

Religion and Psychology

In prayers, in songs, and in dances, in home festivals and synagogue rites, the Jews acted out in unison their own inner needs and passions, finding collective health and enormous powers of resistance as by-products of this wise emotional strategy. The Jewish holydays and festivals in dark ages became substitute therapy for the frustrated and persecuted Jewish soul. The Chasidim of eastern Europe and the builders of modern Palestine, each in their own way, have been wise enough to provide outlets for feeling, as well as for thought, in the worship both of God and of life. It has been much of modern Judaism, under the spell of an idolatrous rationalism, which has tended too often to negate and sterilize the emotional life of contemporary Jews.

Now that Freud has pointed out emotion's power and unyielding dominion, it is for religion to adapt this energy to the uses of good and to make the sanctuary a place where men and women can once again find a brilliant synthesis of feeling and intellect. Through symbolic ceremony and ritual the worshiper can drain off destructive energy and transform it into the life-giving waters of spiritual and ethical reconstruction.

How Religion and Psychiatry Parallel Each Other

How overwhelmingly the similarities between religion and psychiatry heap up at the end of our quest for inward peace!

Tolerance and peace (toward ourselves as well as others) are stressed in both systems. The common brotherhood of man, the universal communion of all races—taught by the prophets of Israel thousands of years ago—are the goals of psychiatric teachers today. The unity of God and the unity of man are parallels drawn by revealed religion and creative psychiatry. And there are countless other parallels. . . .

A prophetic religion like Judaism is future-minded in placing its trust in the Messianic age to redeem the darkness and tragedy of present personal and social failure. Dynamic psychology underscores the intuitive wisdom of religion in stressing the future, because psychology maintains that the human ego lives and grows only when it has a hope for the future—only when there are seeds of new plans in the broken present.

Prophetic religion stresses the importance of faith in the achievement of happiness and inner peace. Here, too, there is a great parallelism between psychology and religion. What does psychoanalysis call for but for mature faith—faith in the possibility of self-mastery and new integration; faith in one's ability to live in accordance with reality principles rather than with pleasure principles; faith in the worthwhileness of fellow human beings and in the possibility of relatedness to them?

Freud has shown that there is much more to human life than the opaque surface of appearance. The belief in the surface of life as the *totality* of life is revealed in all its absurdity through the pioneering efforts of psychoanalysis. We never see our unconscious, yet it works continuously in us. Likewise, we never see God, but the Divine Power continually works in us, undergirds and supports us. Both are invisible, as the electron is invisible, yet they are the most real in ourselves and in the universe—real by the tests of their effects and traces in all of life.

Prophetic religion has eternally taught that in this God-created universe truth is indispensable, and standards and

Religion and Psychology

ideals are inevitable. Throughout this entire volume we have seen how psychology documents these convictions of religion. We have learned how the falsification of our emotional life destroys us, how profoundly we are compelled to tell the truth to ourselves and to others if we desire the victory of love and courage over grief and death.

The words of religion about the nature of life and the universe are not mere Utopian dreams; they are echoes of the best-substantiated facts concerning the nature of reality. Religion comes to man with its rich message of hope that this is a world based upon stable principles of truth, brotherhood, idealism, heroism, love, forgiveness. In a quite independent fashion—and in the language of formulae and equations, rather than of psalms and of prayers—psychology strengthens and verifies these convictions of the sanctuary.

Modern psychology, through its startling new insights into the subtleties and complexities of the human mind, should help religion to modify its views. Untenable interpretations of human nature should be eliminated: morbid traits and attitudes which have been the major obstacles along the road to the good life should be removed. Religion must be brave enough to admit its errors and, after admitting them, use its enormous influence for the creation of a happier and psychically freer mankind. Likewise, religion must be humble enough to accept the tools of the psychological laboratory to force open the door of this final great mystery—why man, with all the power he possesses, is still so far from happiness and peace.

The mystery can be partially solved today by the use of these new insights of dynamic psychology. If man is tormented by an overdemanding conscience; if he has never learned the art of proper self-love, but is enslaved to a compulsive, greedy, never-to-be-satisfied selfishness; if he is driven by inner shadow fears, has never honestly come face to face with grief, nor learned how to transcend it; if he flees from maturity and will not accept adult responsibility—how can such a man ever help to create a good life for himself or a godlike society for others?

How can such a man ever know earthly peace or aspire to the kingdom of heaven?

It is through dynamic psychology that we can, for the first time, understand the emotional inhibitions and distortions which have always prevented men from translating religious ideals into actualities. We know enough now to begin to liberate man. Let us make the attempt upon ourselves; aided by religion, let us engrave upon our hearts the commandments of a new morality:

Thou shalt not be afraid of thy hidden impulses.

Thou shalt learn to respect thyself and then thou wilt love thy neighbor as thyself.

Thou shalt transcend inner anxiety, recognizing thy true competence and courage.

Thou shalt stand undismayed in the presence of grief. Thou shalt not deny the sadness of thy heart. Thou shalt make no detour around sorrow, but shall live through it, and by the aid of human togetherness and comradely sympathy thou shalt win dominion over sorrow.

Thou shalt eternally respect truth and tell it with kindness and also with firmness to all of thy associates, to the young

Religion and Psychology

child as well as to thy brother, and through truth shalt thou find healing and salvation.

Thou shalt search thy heart for the traces of immaturity and the temptations of childishness. Thou shalt reject all flight from freedom, all escape from maturity, as unworthy of thy person. Thou shalt turn away from all supine reliance upon authority, all solacing slavery to an omnipotent social father. Thou shalt seek together with thy brothers a kingdom of mature equality.

Thou shalt uproot from thy heart the false doubts and childish petulance which keep thee far from God. Thou shalt not make Him the scapegoat for thy emotional wounds and thy psychic scars. Thou shalt free thyself of the distortions which block thy way to His presence, and by that freedom thou shalt commune at last with Him, the source of truth, the giver of peace.

ACKNOWLEDGMENTS

PEACE OF MIND has grown out of material first presented as the Charles W. Eliot Lectures at the Jewish Institute of Religion whose great president, Dr. Stephen S. Wise, graciously invited me to present my views on psychology and religion. A number of friends have contributed to make this volume possible.

I am greatly indebted for the inspiration which I have received during these years from my close association and friendship with Dr. Nathan Krass of New York, versatile scholar and great Jewish preacher. I would like particularly to thank my good friend Dr. Roy Grinker of Chicago for first opening up new avenues of psychological insight to me, and likewise to thank my treasured friend, Dr. Solomon Goldman of Chicago, the source of great intellectual stimulation, and to express my gratitude to the distinguished theologian, Professor Mordecai M. Kaplan of the Jewish Theological Seminary in New York for his kindness in reading the manuscript, to my life-long friends, Professor A. N. Franzblau of the Hebrew Union College and his wife Dr. Rose Franzblau for their painstaking and creative help, to the outstanding psychoanalysts, Dr. Edward Bibring and Dr. Grete Bibring for reading the text and making many valuable suggestions, to the brilliant novelist, editor, and essayist, Henry Morton Robinson for his indispensable editorial counsel and guidance, and above all to Dr. Erich Lindemann of Harvard, great psychiatrist and wise friend, who has been an inspiration in this whole project.

I owe a real debt of gratitude also to my secretaries, Enid Rosen Jackson and Bessie R. Berman for their invaluable aid in preparing the manuscript.

ABOUT THE AUTHOR

Dr. Joshua Loth Liebman was not only rabbi of Temple Israel, Boston, but one of the leading radio preachers in America. His sermons over NBC, ABC and CBS coast-to-coast networks were heard by millions, and his Sunday broadcasts to the six New England states had an audience of more than one million listeners.

During the last few years of his life, Dr. Liebman served as University preacher at Harvard, Cornell, Vassar, Dartmouth, Wellesley, Smith, and other leading universities. He was visiting Professor of Jewish Philosophy and Literature at Andover-Newton Theological Seminary. This is believed to be the first time that a rabbi had been invited to become a regular member of a Christian Theological Seminary to teach Judaism to Christian clergymen.

Dr. Liebman studied at the Hebrew University in Jerusalem and the Hebrew Union College in Cincinnati, where he took his doctorate in Jewish philosophy. He was a member of the Governor's Committee on Racial and Religious Understanding for Massachusetts, and was the Chairman of the Governor's Committee of Clergymen. During World War II he served as a member of the Committee on Army and Navy Religious Activities, directing the work of Jewish chaplains.

His death in June 1948 was a shock to the millions whose lives he entered by his teachings.